To Donald and Sheila

With many thanks for your hospitality and friendship.

Love and best wishes

from Ian

King's Lynn and West Norfolk

– History and Landscape –

Text by Paul Richards and Alison Gifford

Paintings by Alan Castleton

Cottage
Publications

First published by Cottage Publications,
an imprint of Laurel Cottage Ltd.
Donaghadee, N. Ireland 2010.
Copyrights Reserved.
© Illustrations by Alan Castleton 2010.
© Text by Paul Richards and Alison Gifford 2010.
All rights reserved.
No part of this book may be reproduced or stored on any media
without the express written permission of the publishers.
Design & origination in Northern Ireland.
Printed & bound in China.
ISBN 978 1 900935 85 2

The Authors

Born and bred in King's Lynn, Paul Richards studied for both BA and PhD degrees in History at Birmingham University followed by teacher training at Nottingham. He taught in further and higher education at the College of West Anglia for 39 years. He has been a part-time tutor for the WEA, Open University and Cambridge, Nottingham and University of East Anglia extra mural departments.

From 1991 to 2003 Paul Richards was a borough councillor (King's Lynn and West Norfolk) and Mayor (1998-2000) before becoming an Honorary Alderman. His *History of King's Lynn* was published in 1990, and he has contributed articles to academic journals and books. Amongst several other interests, he is a trustee of True's Yard Fisherfolk Museum and has been a town guide since 1983.

Alison Gifford moved to King's Lynn as Librarian-in-Charge of the town Library in 1978. The extensive local history collection caught her interest and she started to write and give talks about Lynn history. She has helped to revive the reputation of George Vancouver with her book *Captain George Vancouver of Lynn.* Her *Ghosts and Legends of Lynn* has also been popular along with light-hearted ghost walks.

Alison has also lectured for the WEA on English novels and authors. For nearly ten years she owned and ran a bistro and wine bar in the town. Alison now works for the Norfolk Museum and Archaeological Service and in tourism for the Borough Council.

The Artist

Born in King's Lynn in 1951, the son of a local fisherman, Alan Castleton has spent most of his working life in industry and is now a local businessman actively involved in promoting the best King's Lynn has to offer. Although a native of King's Lynn, at 18 he moved to North Essex where he lived and worked before returning to his King's Lynn roots in 2000.

Painting has always been on a 'time permitting' basis to fit around the demands of work and family with much of the very spasmodic output ending up in private collections or projects for the benefit of charities. He now devotes more of his time to painting and plans to have an exhibition as soon as he has accumulated enough work to fill a venue. Meanwhile, he is happy to take commissions for paintings or illustrations in a variety of mediums.

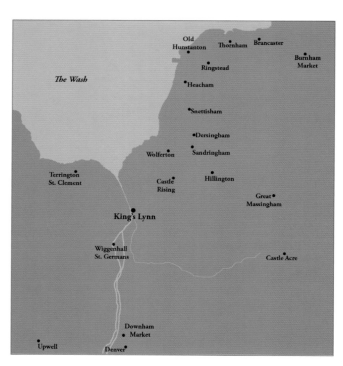

KING'S LYNN AND WEST NORFOLK

Contents

Wonderful West Norfolk: from Flat Fens to High Norfolk

❦

It is said that Norfolk is flat and it is true that there are no real hills and absolutely no mountains. Yet there is an astonishing variety of landscape within this part of western Norfolk. There is sandy breckland, ancient woodland, fir tree forest, seascape, marshland and fen, patchworked by fields and hedges with some undulations called High Norfolk.

The borough of King's Lynn and West Norfolk is about 100 miles from London. Close enough for easy communication and far enough away to be very different. Nearby are Cambridge, Peterborough and Norwich, but King's Lynn is the centre for about 150,000 population from 100 villages and two smaller towns, Hunstanton and Downham Market. It is the fourth largest district in England, covering an area of 550 square miles. Main roads run through from Leicester to Great Yarmouth and via Ely and Cambridge to London though the direct electrified main line railway is a much better way to travel. Our port has sea links to northern and eastern Europe and that has been the case for a thousand years. Over all this presides the Mayor and Corporation of the Borough and the towns of Hunstanton and Downham Market also have a Mayor and Town Council known collectively and colloquially when gathered together as the Chain Gang.

Heritage, history and sea are the wonderful combination that make West Norfolk special. To the west the low-lying land and sea merge so when you gaze out towards the Wash at no point can you exactly discern where the sea is, or is not, or where the land begins and ends. West Norfolk is sky country. Huge skies dominate; torn clouds scattered with skeins of honking geese, sunsets of breathtaking beauty, and a luminescent blue dome over all on lovely summer days. We have an easy climate; trouble, if it comes, comes from the sea. The Wash is a great arc punched into the coast marbled by stealthily shifting sands with ancient and evocative names; Pandora, Thief, Blackguard Seal, Westmark Knock, Black Dog, Gat and Roaring Middle. The tides steal up quietly and quickly to cover the coastal salt marshes, which can surprise amateur samphire pickers, an activity best left to hardy locals who gather this succulent marsh weed from early summer to late July. But when the weather changes and the wind is from the north, sweeping in from Siberia, great waves crash onto the beaches at Heacham, dashing against the sea walls and falling ferociously onto the cliffs at Hunstanton, scouring the sands and dunes at Holme-next-

the-Sea and Brancaster. Then, when the sun shines and the sea is as calm as a lake with myriad pecking birds on the shore and mudflats and marram grass climbing very gently up to lovely, heathy and wooded chalk land dotted with modest towered churches of the villages of Great and Little Massingham, Docking, Stiffkey, Harpley and all the little village communities of West Norfolk, all is well.

Very little landscape here has drama but within the borough there is variety and charm. The local carrstone and flint cottages, occasional windmills and some very fine stately houses at the end of long deserted roads are the backbone of this countryside. A few grand landowners own most of the land and the farms. The Queen at Sandringham is probably the best known. Barley, rape, linseed and sugar beet are staple crops and pigs, sheep, geese and turkeys are the livestock. To the west on the rich black loam of marshland and fenland bloom tulips, daffodils, roses and cauliflowers. Potatoes, cabbages and big fat orange pumpkins thrive. Agricultural abundance has not always been the case here; not only did time, effort and money have to be spent on the drainage of the fens but luckily the greatest agricultural pioneers of the age were West Norfolk land owners. Charles 'Turnip' Townsend of Raynham (1674-1738) and Coke of Leicester at Holkham (1754-1842) changed farming practises. The barren Holkham estate had 'one blade of grass and two rabbits fighting for it', no cattle, little corn and only

800 sheep on 3000 acres. The trouble was light, blowy soil. Thomas William Coke dug into the underlying marl (clay) and spread it on the top. He followed the four course rotation of crops pioneered by his turnip-growing neighbour and the sheep which cleared the leftover root crop manured the fields, 'four footed muck spreaders'. The land prospered and the estate became a rich model for farmers from all over eastern England.

There were probably more tracks and green roads in ancient times than we can now imagine and these rights of way have been gradually eroded although our modern network of roads owe their origins to our Roman, Anglo-Saxon and Medieval legacy. The conquering Romans found a landscape marked by crossroads of innumerable tracks along which the first expeditionary Roman forces must have carried out their exploration and reconnaissance. A Roman measurement was one thousand paces of a military cohort, a *mille passum,* now our mile. The Peddars Way is the earliest Roman road in the county built under military supervision. Local people must have been the main labour force but we do not know if labour was actually forced or if native labour was 'contracted out' after training. Whatever stood in the way mattered not, a wide belt of land was cleared and the road was built. We know there was a reliance on local material, stone and gravel, but have no archaeological indication of any quarries. There have been three phases of road building in Norfolk that have been planned and not haphazard; Roman, turnpike and bypass.

Early signposts were wayside crosses and a few survivals may be seen, at Pentney for example. Money from the sale of church goods at the Reformation paid for improved roads, bridges, causeways and a system of beacons. Beacon Hill near Hunstanton was the site of one. At one time many of our coastal villages were thriving ports, for example Burnham Overy was visited by kogges, barges, schooners, brigs and brigantines bringing coal, timber, wine, wax and taking barley, malt and cloth round the coast and into the Baltic until the tides dumped so much sand and shingle as to make the little seaport landbound. Then Overy Staithe was built as an outport until the coming of the railways finished that commerce. 'Staithe' means landing place or stage and is one of the many Viking words and names found all over West Norfolk. Water transport was vitally important for moving heavy goods until the railways changed the economy and society of West Norfolk, and when the railway lines were short-sightedly axed in the late 1950s, our inevitable reliance on road transport has brought its own problems.

Tourism is essential to the economy of West Norfolk. Visitors can walk the Peddars Way and Norfolk Coastal Path, using the excellent Coasthopper bus between villages.

West Norfolk has a very good bus service connecting up all the main towns and larger villages. Records show that Frank Morriss, owner of The Sandringham Motor Garage in London Road, King's Lynn, started one of the first bus services. In 1900 this clever and imaginative engineering entrepreneur built an omnibus to his own design which ran from the South Gate to the Swan Inn at Gaywood. He sold very upmarket cars as well and one of his customers was Edward VII when he was resident at Sandringham. Visitors who want to avoid roads can hop on the ferry at Lynn to West Lynn to start the Peter Scott Walk – named for the renowned bird expert, painter and naturalist who lived on these lonely marshes – walk the Fen Rivers Way or ramble the Nar valley, popping into Narborough Mill and Trout Farm for some pink fleshed fresh trout, and venture out by boat to see the seals at Scolt Head. They can windsurf or sail and enjoy effortless cycling on minor roads and cycleways. They can see the Queen's private sitting room at Sandringham, Walpole's great marble hall at Houghton and at Castle Rising the Maison Forte where Queen Isabella, the She Wolf of France, was kept in luxurious semi-captivity.

Children and Hunstanton are made for each other.

NARBOROUGH MILL

A circle of 55 timber posts surrounding an upturned oak tree root stump were revealed at Holme-next-the-Sea in 1998 when the coastal sand shifted as it has since time immemorial. This mysterious object may have remained unconsidered, washed away or silted over again, but exposure in the press made intervention inevitable as hundreds of sightseers unknowingly trampled over sensitive marshes – a site of Special Scientific Interest – to see it. A difficult and controversial removal of the timbers attracted national attention. Half the timber circle and the tree root are now in the Lynn Museum. They are dated to the Bronze Age, 2400 BC, but what their reason for being or their use is utterly unknown.

Houghton Hall is the biggest country house in Norfolk. It was built in Palladian style and designed by William Kent for Sir Robert Walpole, M.P. for King's Lynn, who was regarded as the first Prime Minister. It was begun in 1721 and finished in 1735. There have been three houses on this site but this last is superlative; splendid, expensive, big, sumptuous and all executed with fine craftsmanship. It had so many paintings it was sneeringly called 'The National Gallery' but that all changed when dissolute, possibly mad, George Walpole (1730-1791) sold the paintings to Catherine the Great of Russia. The estate came through the female line to the Cholmondeley family.

Legal hunting and shooting has always been the leisure pursuit of the privileged rich upper classes. When poor village men tried the same hunting and shooting for their family pot and were caught by the gamekeeper employed by the landlord, they were likely to be tried by that same land-owning magistrate and their punishment could be prison or transportation. The nineteenth century was a heyday for organised shooting parties gathering for the weekend at country houses. Col. Hawker recalls a time when the Marquis of Ripon, shooting at Sandringham, killed 28 pheasants in one minute.

But if game was not forthcoming, what could be better than a Norfolk dumpling. Norfolk is the county for dumplings. Those made with yeast are known as 'floaters' and those made with suet as 'sinkers'. Norfolk dumplings should always be torn apart; cutting them will make them heavy, not fluffy, and served as a first course with rich brown onion gravy. Or fish; with over fifty miles of coastline bordering the county, fishing has given local people many interesting and tasty dishes. West Norfolk does shellfish; cockles, mussels, oysters and pink and brown shrimps. There are very few actual fish in the Wash because the seals eat them all. The bounty of the seas combined with the harvest of the land has exactly suited the tenor of the times with a surge of interest in wholesome traditional local food simply cooked. Town restaurants and a growing number of village pubs with very good food are welcome to locals and visitors alike.

There is an attractive group of seven Burnham villages on the Norfolk coast. They are Deepdale, Market, Norton, Overy, Sutton, Thorpe and Ulph. The most popular is Burnham Market, a picturesque village with fine handsome Georgian houses round a green where a little brook runs over the street. The most famous is Burnham Thorpe, the birthplace of Norfolk hero, Admiral Lord Nelson.

The charming rectory where Horatio Nelson was born on 29th September 1758 has gone but the village, the mile long lane to the church, the cottages, farms and fields are still as Nelson knew them as a boy. He left home to go to sea on his uncle's ship when he was 12. His father, Edmund, who was rector here until his death in 1802, had a family of nine with Horatio the 4th child and 3rd son. His closest sibling was his brother William, eighteen months older, who would, on the 21st October 1805 when Lord Nelson died at the Battle of Trafalgar, be catapulted from his Norfolk parsonage house at Hilborough to inherit the title of Lord Nelson of the Nile, Burnham Thorpe and Brontë. A grateful Parliament, bereft of the nation's true hero, then made him an Earl, gave him £100,000 and a huge house renamed Trafalgar House.

The church at Burnham Thorpe which serves the parish is also a memorial to Lord Nelson and the Nelson family. By the porch are the ledger stones of his eldest brother

Maurice Nelson and sister Susannah Bolton. By the altar are the memorials of his mother Catherine and father Edmund. Catherine Nelson was related to the Walpole family and her elaborate gravestone is a statement of her almost aristocracy. The village pub, The Lord Nelson, formerly The Plough, is also full of Nelson memorabilia but otherwise the village has remained unexploited by tearooms and souvenir shops.

When Nelson was killed at the Battle of Trafalgar, his status as a national hero superseded his wish written in a letter to a Norfolk neighbour:

'Probably I shall never see dear dear Burnham again but I have the satisfaction of thinking my bones will probably be laid with my father's in the village that gave me birth. Pardon my dear Sir this digression but the thoughts of former days brings all my mother into my heart which shows itself in my eyes'.

His bones lie in St. Paul's Cathedral.

To the south of the borough are inland waterways where little cruisers huddle against the banks of the Little Ouse, the Nar and the Whissey, and straddling the River Great Ouse is the imposing Denver Sluice through which all the boats, yachts, barges and narrowboats must go, using locks to navigate from the Lynn Ouse into the Ely Ouse. This mighty feat of engineering regulates the water of the Great Ouse. The wealth of goods pouring from the port of Lynn for hundreds of years were taken down this waterway by the old bargees and lightermen which brought them into conflict with the fenland drainers and the farmers. Then the railways came and gave them all a big surprise.

For hundreds of years the pace of life was slow and traditional, the seasons of the year came round reflecting the repetition and rhythm of religious life. Norfolk has more medieval churches than any other English county, a feast of modest round-towered churches, some huge rich churches rising from the fens like cathedrals and the remains of friaries, priories, nunneries and monasteries scatter the countryside especially in the part called 'Norfolk's Holy Land' whose life blood was the River Nar. Across the West Norfolk countryside came pilgrims, landing at Lynn and walking along the Pilgrims Way to Walsingham, to the Shrine of Our Lady. The jewel in the crown of this mini Holy Land is Castle Acre with its great Cluniac Priory and, of course, castle. This village is overwhelmingly pretty but has a Norfolk pragmatism in its modern bungalows and council housing which still make it a living community, a pattern reflected in many Norfolk villages. But second homes and holiday lets have blighted many coastal communities. Post offices have closed, the pub has gone, commuting villagers, holiday makers and second homers neglect the village shop and patronise supermarkets in nearby towns. Traditional village institutions of the public house, Women's Institute, and Horticultural Society, of shop and church and knowing your neighbour seem to be failing. Yet some villages have reorganised themselves into a new cohesive community with Local History Societies publishing books, making CDs, holding talks and lectures, bringing cinema to the village hall and keen beer drinkers volunteering to buy and run the local pub.

West Norfolk has always been spread-out, open, defenceless and vulnerable to waves of invaders and settlers. Romans, Vikings, Normans and the Dutch have left their mark on the landscape and traditions and in our village names. Neither Napoleon nor Hitler managed to sneak ashore but that fear was very real and invasion very possible. The flat land was ideal for airfields in the two World Wars and hundreds of aircraft flew sorties over occupied Europe and Germany. West Norfolk was home to hundreds of young men. Americans in the Forces stationed here married local girls who are now great grandmothers keeping up links and visits to their Norfolk relations. Challenges and change are again presented by people migrating from Eastern Europe and Portugal attracted by jobs in the fertile fens and associated food factories.

Royal Airforce Station Marham, 10 miles south of King's Lynn, is home to No 138 Expeditionary Air Wing and is one of the RAF's main operating bases. Four squadrons of Tornado GR4/GR4A Aircraft and six Wings are currently deployed out of Marham. RAF Marham opened in 1916 on an 80 acre site close to the former Royal Navy Air Station at Narborough as a military night landing ground. The aerodrome was closed in 1919 but with war clouds looming, it was reopened and reconstructed in 1935. In 1944 Marham constructed a new concrete runway ready for its post war operations. During 1977 24 Hardened Aircraft Shelters were built each holding 4 WE177 nuclear bombs for the Tornados. The RAF ended its nuclear mission in the United Kingdom by 1998. In action during the Falklands War in 1982 was a large detachment of Victor K2 tankers based at Ascension Island supporting bombing missions. The Gulf War in early 1991 saw RAF Marham squadrons deployed to liberate Kuwait. The personnel from Marham have flown in conflicts in Iraq, Bosnia and Afghanistan and returned from all these war zones to great acclaim. RAF Marham is embedded into the local community of West Norfolk with residents accepting the noisy low flying and bombing raids into the Wash essential to keeping the crew operational. RAF Marham has the Freedom of the Borough of King's Lynn and West Norfolk. The station crest is a glaring blue bull and the motto is 'Deter'.

More recently Londoners and others have escaped urban life to settle in this countryside. Many people will remember when the little rail station at Watlington was called Magdalen Road and the name was cut into the hedge to complement the colourful station flower beds. The station opened in 1846 on the line from Lynn to London where a junction also branched to Wisbech which closed, along with the station, in 1969. Local efforts re-opened the station as Magdalen Road in 1975 with a name change to Watlington in 1989. The original station building on the southbound side has been converted to a private house. When a popular movement pushed for the electrification of the line to London, a housing building boom in the village followed a tremendous demand from commuters for local houses. Well over 100,000 people use the station each year. Dr Beeching would be perplexed.

If our ancestors could come again into West Norfolk they would find much altered but very much to recognise in the churches, cottages, hedgerows and copses, pediments and gables and the long stretches of coast and sand dunes. If they could ignore the cars and bland modern suburbs, the ugly retail parks and deserted second homes then, in the neat villages and historic towns, in the black peat of the fens, the many rivers and waterways and the prosperous farms they would find much to delight in still under our wide high sky.

This is the largest of all the Burnhams lying in a wooded hollow sheltered from the sea. The green, bisected by a broad village street and a little brook called Goose Beck, is an imposing approach to the church of St. Mary and around are gathered splendid and attractive Georgian houses, inns and small shops. At the other end of the green is All Saints' Church representing the decayed village of Burnham Ulph, for Burnham Market, unusually, now covers three parishes. The ruins of St. Ethelbert of Burnham Sutton are nearby. The establishment of a successful market in the Middle Ages in competition with local contenders led to the development of an urban community and town bigger than the surrounding agricultural villages.

The principal inn in this handsome little town is the Hoste Arms, renamed for Sir William Hoste (1780-1828) who was Nelson's favourite protégé and professional heir. Nelson took to sea for his last twelve years of mounting fame several Norfolk boys to be 'captain's servants' and trained as officers. It is said Nelson gave young William Hoste a frigate command and sent him off on an errand so he would survive the battle which finally took place at Trafalgar. William Hoste's glittering career inspired the character of Horatio Hornblower made famous by the seafaring novels of C.S. Forester.

Horatia, Nelson's daughter by Lady Hamilton, came to settle as a young woman in Burnham Market with her uncle's family. She had been with her mother who died of poverty and alcohol in Calais and was brought back to England by the Nelson family with whom she lived until her marriage to Philip Ward, a curate and next-door neighbour here.

The inn is the centre of an odd phenomenon where Burnham Market has become the favourite Norfolk destination of well-to-do Londoners and television people who have, in turn, attracted restaurants, delicatessens, boutiques, interior decorating businesses and art shops to the town.

Burnham Market

WEST NORFOLK

Roman ruler, British subject and Saxon pirate knew Brancaster (Branodunum) as a base of operations for Rome's fleet protecting the approaches to the Wash and its corn growing hinterland. Some archaeologists believe land division of a type found in Italy has survived in the local landscape patterns of today and the hedges, ditches and tracks are the remains of Roman farms. The most popular game bird on Norfolk estates is the pheasant brought from Italy to stock the hen houses of these Anglo-Roman villas. Apicius, writing about 250 AD, gives instructions on how to raise these birds and prepare and cook them for the table. In the last decades of fading Roman rule Anglo-Saxons increasingly menaced the shore and a great fortress was built of which nothing remains, but in 1600 reports were of walls standing 12 feet high. Today a combination of salt marshes, creeks and dunes has formed between this fort site and Brancaster bay.

The parish of Brancaster comprises Brancaster itself, Brancaster Staithe and Burnham Deepdale, forming almost continuous settlement along the coast between Hunstanton and Wells-next-the-Sea. Brancaster Staithe is a picturesque working fishing village in an Area of Outstanding Natural Beauty. The clean waters of the bay make it an ideal area for fishing mussels, lobsters and crabs which can be bought fresh from wooden beach shops close to the Jolly Sailors public house.

The Royal West Norfolk Golf Club is squeezed between Brancaster bay and the salt marshes. It was formed in 1892 and almost nothing has changed in 100 years on these classic links and in the clubhouse. The golf course has a narrow strip of links-land which is cut off at high tide making a round both interesting and wet.

Brancaster Staithe is also home to a busy and popular Sailing Club which is at the forefront of dingy sailing with races every weekend from Easter to October.

Brancaster

WEST NORFOLK

Alan Castleton.

The village of Thornham is separated from the sea by a mile of marshes. This part of the Norfolk coast has constantly changed and shifted over generations and now the land is winning a battle with the sea as silting fills up channels and forces it further from the villages. The once thriving little ports along this coast with their natural bays and estuaries gradually slipped into decline in the 18th century, except for local shell fishing, a flurry of activity each autumn when the barley harvest was shipped out to local malting houses and the smuggling trade.

Thornham was the scene of a notorious battle in 1782 between a smuggling gang led by Thomas Franklyn whose members included most of the village, and Excise Officer Robert Bliss and his five officers over some smuggled tea. The battle was bloody and the Excise men only just escaped with their lives. Most coastal churchyards have someone buried there who was done to death on one side or another of the smuggling wars. Although Customs are of immemorial age, Excise was not introduced until the Civil War to provide money for the parliamentary forces. Customs are money paid on the import of certain goods; wine, tobacco and spirits are some examples, and Excise is money raised again when these goods are sold. Later the revenue from this tax was handed back to be part of the income of Charles II. He paid Nell Gwynn £500 a month from this revenue to enjoy her company.

So prevalent was smuggling around Thornham and so involved were most of the population that conviction of smugglers by a local jury was impossible. Even murderers were acquitted. Often the smuggler has been portrayed as a romantic figure, but during wars, the Napoleonic for example, they committed acts of treason by running the blockade and buying brandy in return for giving the French assistance with a supply of English newspapers, news of the building of fortifications and the deposition of our fleet.

Off the coast of Thornham are the stumps of a petrified prehistoric forest which show how dramatic changes to landscape and coast are through the ages.

Thornham

WEST NORFOLK

Alan Castleton

The attractive village of carrstone and flint at the end of a charming valley where the flat coast country of the Wash rises to the windswept downs was once known as Great Ringstead. Little Ringstead died away in the Black Death of 1349-1350 leaving only a ruinous church. The village that survived had itself two churches up to 1771 when most of St. Peter's was pulled down and the building material used to mend the other parish church of St. Andrews. The remains of St. Peter's round tower are still in the garden of a nice Georgian former rectory house and at one time made a very good dovecot.

The coast nearby was ravaged by Vikings from about AD 800 and it is probable that our Ringstead is a place name from Denmark where Ringsted is a thriving city in the centre of the Island of Zealand. Some sources say Ringstead is Old English and the site of a disappeared sacred ring of wood or stone.

Through Ringstead drives the Peddars Way; the best-known, most substantial and best surviving Roman road in Norfolk, dead straight from its sketchy start near Thetford. It is probably military in origin and reaches the coast at Holme-next-the-Sea where it is reasonable to conjecture that a ferry sailed across the mouth of the Wash to Lincolnshire and then by boat using the inland rivers to Lincoln and York. It would have saved weeks on a land journey across fenland westwards around the Wash.

Courtyard Farm covers 750 acres and was one of the first farms in Norfolk to convert to organic methods of crop and animal production in the 1970s by avoiding artificial fertilisers and pesticides. The farm aims to combine profitable farming while promoting an environment where native wildlife and insects can thrive. The rare breeds of pigs and cattle are kept in conditions as close to their natural habitat as possible and visitors are encouraged to explore the farm.

Two notable landmarks in Ringstead are the remains of an unusual six-sailed brick tower mill and the well known 17th century pub with rooms, the Gin Trap, where the local Morris men and women gather for traditional dances on occasion.

Ringstead

WEST NORFOLK

Alan Castleton

The village of Old Hunstanton creeps towards a towering 60 ft cliff which is banded white and reddish brown of chalk and local carrstone. It looks west, uniquely of east coast holiday resorts, over a wonderful sandy beach strewn with seaweed, rocks, mussel beds and rock pools. The sea is the Wash which, as its name suggests, comes and goes over great tracts of sand with stealthy rapidity. The Lincolnshire coast and the soaring high tower of St. Botolph's Church, Boston, can be seen across the Wash on a clear day when every evening brings the most glorious sunsets. Here St. Edmund, the first Saxon King of East Anglia, landed and today we see the scanty remains of his chapel.

The lighthouse, built in 1840, is the third one on this site and is now a private house. The first one burnt down – it was made of wood and the light was a coal fire. Ezekiel Walker built the second lighthouse in 1778 which similarly used a coal fire but, magnified by his invention of 18 reflectors, the light could be seen 15 miles away. He died aged 94 in 1834 and his memorial is in St. James Park cemetery, King's Lynn.

HUNSTANTON CLIFFS

Hunstanton has attracted families on holiday since a new town was planted in 1846 by local landowner and squire, Henry Styleman Le Strange (1815-1862), a successful speculation at the beginning of the railway age to build a new resort. It remains a deeply Victorian town with notable carrstone houses centred round a green and, at one time, a fine pier which was damaged by fire and finally washed away in 1978. The gentrification of New Hunstanton was complete when Edward VII visited from nearby Sandringham after his recovery from typhoid fever in 1871. Today Hunstanton is still a very busy holiday town from Easter until October with the townspeople welcoming visitors but it is also a thriving community with clubs, talks, exhibitions and festivals. The town still has its own mayor and council.

The railway has gone of course, short-sightedly closed down in 1969.

Old Hunstanton

WEST NORFOLK

Alan Castleton

The village of Heacham is very nearly a small town with extensive beaches along the shores of the Wash about fourteen miles from King's Lynn so has a seasonal population of holidaymakers, mostly in caravan parks.

In the church at Heacham is a fine alabaster portrait of Pocohontas, the Native American Princess, by Otillea Wallace, a pupil of Rodin. John Rolfe of Heacham and John Smith, an apprentice in Lynn, were headhunted by Walter Raleigh to sail to Virginia as early colonisers. Rolfe sailed in 1609 with his wife in the *Sea Venture* which became separated from the rest of the fleet and was wrecked on the Bermuda Islands. The crew of the *Sea Venture* made two new boats from cedar wood and reached Jamestown safely. Three accounts were quickly written of this adventure and it seems certain that Shakespeare had read one which was his inspiration for *The Tempest*.

Near starvation conditions in the new colony took their toll and Mrs Rolfe died. Without the support of the local Native American tribes the colony would have starved to death. John Rolfe and John Smith knew the great king Pohowtan and were smitten by his daughter Pocohontas but a gunpowder accident forced badly injured John Smith back to England and John Rolfe married the beautiful princess in 1613. They came to London where the queen and court received them with delight. A son, Thomas, was born in 1615 but Pocohontas died of small pox while at Gravesend waiting for a ship to return to Virginia. Thomas Rolfe is the ancestor of many famous families in the United States. The Rolfe family was associated with Heacham until 1941 when Heacham Hall burnt down.

Also in the church is a brass of 1799 which tells of nine people who went boating on a Sunday and drowned; *'a warning to rising and future generations against rashly engaging in similar undertakings'.*

The fields of lavender are characteristic around Heacham in early July when the scent fills the air and a prosperous industry at Caley Mill, on the main Lynn to Hunstanton road, harvests the lavender to make the famous Norfolk Lavender products.

View towards Heacham

WEST NORFOLK

Just inland from the coast but with its own beach is the very interesting village of Snettisham. It is pretty, large and nicely situated on this well wooded coast with the feel of a small market town reflecting its more important past. The carrstone dominating the traditional building material is quarried here. Snettisham has the finest Norfolk church of the decorated period which would be larger if the old decayed chancel had not been taken down in Elizabeth I's reign. The spire of St. Mary's, unusual in West Norfolk, soars to 175 feet and was a seamark for sailors.

There must have been some very wealthy people living here in the first century who made extraordinary lavish ornaments and jewellery from precious metals. In particular they made 'torcs' which are a front opening neck decoration. A hoard of torcs have been found in Snettisham and more torcs and bracelets have been found in Norfolk than in any other part of the country. The Snettisham Great Torc, which is dated from the Iron Age at 75 AD, is the most elaborate object made at this time in the ancient world; it is a kilogram of gold and silver minutely twisted to form ropes which are again twisted into moulded finials. The Great Torc, now in the British Museum, was ploughed up with other artefacts on the local estate of Ken Hill. Sir Edward Green commissioned this stylish mansion in 1879-80 on a hill overlooking the Wash, now the Royal Society for the Preservation of Birds reserve which is very popular with migrating birds and their human watchers.

It seems extraordinary that a West Norfolk village has the distinction of being the first place bombed from the air in the history of the world but it so happened to Snettisham on 19th January 1915 by German Zeppelin airship no LZ27 (L4). Apparently three Zeppelins were pathfinders to London following the railway line from Lynn to London once they had crossed the North Sea but they turned the wrong way towards Hunstanton and mistook Snettisham Church for Ely Cathedral; no doubt the sight of the Wash a few minutes later was quite a surprise.

Dr W. G. Grace, the legendary cricket player, holidayed here in the early 1900s with his friend who was headmaster of a little grammar school domesticated in a house called The Halls.

Snettisham

WEST NORFOLK

AlanCastleton

Dersingham is a large populous and popular village about 7 miles north of King's Lynn. Among the 4,500 inhabitants is a large proportion of well-to-do retired people so bungalows are mixed in with the traditional carrstone cottages. It is a self-reliant village with a complete range of shops and services but the adventurous will find that the bus service is good and links up with the train to Cambridge and London from King's Lynn.

It is the largest village on the Royal Sandringham Estate. The Feathers Hotel, a well-known pub and restaurant, was bought by the Prince of Wales in 1882. The feathers are the three Prince of Wales feathers which are painted on the pub sign.

A large fine tithe barn stands next to the big church of St. Nicholas in the centre of the old village. It is carrstone and red brick dated 1671. The tithe was an annual payment of an agreed proportion, originally one tenth, of the yearly produce of the land in a parish given to support the parish church and its clergyman. Tithes were either great or small. Great tithes were corn, hay, other grains and wood which were stored in the barn. Milk, eggs, wool and a percentage of profits from fishing and milling were small tithes. Thus the rector's standard of living varied from parish to parish. In 1836 the Tithe Commutation Act was passed with Commissioners appointed to set a monetary payment instead of 'in kind' all over the country. One excellent result is the series of tithe maps produced which give us a detailed view of our historic rural landscape.

Dersingham bog is a wilderness area owned by English Nature where some very rare species survive, so rare that the much hoped for bypassing of this village, oppressed with holiday traffic travelling bumper to bumper to Hunstanton in the summer for years, was on hold for a short time. The villagers are fonder of the rare moth *buckleria paludum* now than they were then.

Dersingham

WEST NORFOLK

Alan Castleton

In 1846 Charles Spencer Cowper, at the age of 30, had been left both Beachamwell and Sandringham estates by John Motteaux, an eccentric wealthy bachelor. Motteaux was a close intimate of the Cowper family from his long friendship with the 5th Earl Cowper, and his gay manners, overblown generosity and obsession with all things gastronomic was a source of wry amusement to London Society who, nevertheless, accepted his fine hospitality.

Spencer Cowper, his heir, was born in 1816. Emily Cowper reputedly had her 5 children by various men. *'Palmerston may have been the father of some of her children and another is said to be the child of Pozzo di Borgo, a Corsican Friend of Napoleon's'.* Cowper lost no time in selling the Beachamwell estate in order to rent a grand house and fund an extravagant life in London and Paris. His care of Sandringham and its tenants was negligible but, nevertheless, he held the offices expected of his class and position becoming Deputy-Lieutenant and then High Sheriff of Norfolk. But Cowper was in financial trouble. Bored by Sandringham, he must have been delighted when Lord Palmerston dextrously negotiated the sale of Sandringham to the Prince of Wales. In 1862 the Prince of Wales paid a fantastic £220,000 for *'a shooting box'.* The choice of Sandringham was extraordinary, as observed by Lady Macclesfield;

'Here are numerous coverts, but no fine woods, large unenclosed turnip fields with an occasional haystack to break the line of the horizon. It would be difficult to find a more ugly or desolate looking place, and there is no neighbourhood or any other countervailing advantage. The wind blows from the Wash and the Spring is said to be unendurable in this part of Norfolk. It is, of course, a wretched hunting country and it is dangerous riding as the banks are honeycombed with rabbit holes. As there was all England to choose I do wish they had a finer house in a more cheerful situation'.

Now a fine prosperous estate of 20,000 acres the care and influence of the Royal Family have changed the land, house and welfare of the tenants and estate workers very much for the better.

Charles Spencer Cowper died from a fever at Albano in Italy in 1879.

In front of the stables at Sandringham House is an equestrian statue of *Persimmon* (1893 – 1908), an outstanding thoroughbred racehorse, which was owned by the Prince of Wales. *Persimmon* won the Derby and many other races, earning the Prince £34,706 before his career as a successful sire. This 1896 Derby was the first horse race ever filmed.

Sandringham

WEST NORFOLK

PERSIMMON

Alan Castleton

This pretty, well-kept village is part of the Sandringham Royal Estate and royal influence has long been evident. In 1886 Edward, Prince of Wales, who was an enthusiastic local landowner, extensively restored St. Peter's Church. By the entrance to the Church is an outrageous ultra-gothic bookcase of German origin which came from Windsor Castle. Whether the Royals liked it so much they brought it to Norfolk or really hated it and dumped it with dignity we have no record.

Wolferton's best-known building is its fine Victorian Tudor Gothic railway station and station master's house of carrstone. It was opened in 1863, a year after Edward, Prince of Wales, purchased the Sandringham Estate with income from the Duchy of Cornwall. A couple of months later, the Prince and Alexandra of Denmark came as a newly married couple to this country station to begin the Royal Family's long association with West Norfolk. The building is a delight with royal touches all over; crowns surmount the lamps and the waiting room, sitting room and oak panelled snug are fit for a king, and indeed the royalty of Europe passed through this station from Willem II to the Tsar Nicholas. Queen Victoria visited Sandringham in 1889 and arrived at Wolferton where the West Norfolk Hunt acted as an escort to the royal residence while hundreds of people thronged the route. The line became too busy for the single track to cope by the 1890s so another track was laid and a downside station built. Between 1884 and 1911, 645 royal trains steamed in and out of Wolferton station. A sad journey in 1952 took the body of George VI to London after his death at Sandringham. The line from Lynn to Hunstanton through Wolferton closed in 1966 after which the station became a museum, but in 2001 it was bought as a private house.

There is a royal stud in the village and local people are quite used to the Queen driving herself to see the horses and especially the newborn foals. A race at Royal Ascot named the Wolferton Handicap Stakes was added to the race meeting to celebrate the Queen's Golden Jubilee in 2002.

Wolferton

WEST NORFOLK

WOL FERTON

Alan Castleton

Castle Rising lies on a bypassed road from King's Lynn to Hunstanton so it is now a peaceful village gently slumbering in genteel old age but 800 years ago it was a youthful bustling port and market. So important was Castle Rising before the sea retreated that it became a famous rotten borough, sending two members to parliament and electing a High Steward, Mayor, Recorder, 12 Aldermen and 50 Burgesses when there were only 60 voters. Samuel Pepys was an M.P. for Castle Rising in 1673. It was almost impossible for the men of Castle Rising not to hold civic office, be they ever so humble. This continued until the parliamentary reform of 1832. The 20 foot high market cross on the village green shows how busy this village once was on market day. It is 15th century but by 1600 the market *hath almost expired the Ghost* which was a common fate amongst the many village markets as easier travel and competition weeded out the smaller ones.

The castle was originally an impressive Norman stronghold built by William d'Albini, 1st Earl of Arundel, but by 1330 it was really a Maison Forté, a posh fortified house of the time. It was neither strong enough to be a true castle nor in a part of the country likely to be attacked, but it was ideally suited to keep Queen Isabella of France in loose and luxurious captivity to atone for her crime of murdering her weak effeminate husband, King Edward II, and giving Geoffrey Mortimer, her lover, too much power. Edward III, her son, had to appear to punish her but in fact she had freedom to go for Christmas visits, hunting and visiting the Franciscan friars at Lynn. The King and her grandson, the Black Prince, visited occasionally and had to be lavishly feasted to the dismay of the Corporation accountant in Lynn who had to pay the bills.

The Bede House given by Henry Howard, Earl of Northampton, is a very pleasing almshouse built in 1614 for 12 *'poore women'* and their governess. There are still worthy ladies living here who wear Jacobean red cloaks and pointed steeple hats to church and on Founder's Day. The late Norman Church of St. Lawrence has an unusual Victorian saddleback roof but the striking west front with its round arched doorway enriched with bold zig-zag moulding is a lasting tribute to its early builders.

The harmony of these, and other attractive buildings and houses, make Castle Rising one of our prettiest Norfolk villages.

Castle Rising

WEST NORFOLK

Alan Castleton

Hillington is a village largely built of local carrstone on the Lynn to Cromer A148 road. About 300 people live here. Two buildings catch the eye; the lodges and gatehouse of Hillington Hall and the Ffolkes Arms Hotel. The original hall was Jacobean of 1627 built for Sir Richard Hovell. He had the miserable task of being one of the Lynn burgesses who surrendered that town to the Parliamentary forces of the Earl of Manchester after a siege from 28th August to 15th September 1643. This caused by Lynn's Mayor and Corporation, after months of vacillation, declaring for the King, Charles I, during the Civil War. After much alteration in 1824 the hall was pulled down in 1947. Martin Ffolkes married Dorothy Hovell in 1678 and the estate passed into the Ffolkes family whose marriages and financial interests grew to involve almost every gentry family of West Norfolk. The fine gatehouse was erected in 1831, built from the old stones of the demolished Market Cross at Lynn (built 1710) which was designed by local architect Henry Bell of Custom House fame. The stones cost Sir W. J. M. B. Ffolkes £160.

The Ffolkes Arms hotel was built as a hunting lodge and was often used into the early 20th century by the Royal Family from Sandringham about 3 miles away while they shot most of the local pheasant population. East Anglia was, at one period, covered in forests which sheltered innumerable deer and boars legally hunted by the rich but, when poached by the poor, a dangerous criminal activity. Forests, usually about 200 acres, were areas where common law did not apply, only the King's law mattered and the King owned all the forests in the land unless he granted the forest to a subject when it became a 'chase'. We learn that Sir Roger Townshend had a chase that extended from *'Gaywood Brigge to the See, from thence to Babingley Brigge from thence to Hillington Brigge'* in 1543.

The Queen always attends one Sunday morning service at St. Mary's Church, Hillington, during her Sandringham Christmas break.

Hillington Hall

Gatelodge

WEST NORFOLK

Alan Castleton .

There are two Massinghams, Little and Great. The larger has as much water as green and quite a lot of both. Between the two greens is the fine church of St. Mary's. The four large duck ponds were fish pools of the 11th century Augustinian Abbey which was 'surrendered', that is seized by Henry VIII zealots, in 1538 but fragments of it exist in the house and outbuildings of Abbey Farm. No doubt it was a rich house as there is evidence that Edward I stayed on 29th March 1302 on his way to the Shrine of Our Lady at Walsingham.

William Bewley, the 'Philosopher of Massingham' (1726-1783), a surgeon apothecary of humble means and education, was a native of Great Massingham. He is best known for his articles produced for the *Monthly Review*. He corresponded with many eminent thinkers of the day including the chemist Joseph Priestly who wrote that *'the review of my History of Electricity by Mr Bewley was the means of opening a correspondence between us, which was the source of much satisfaction'*. Bewley was a particular friend of Charles Burney, the musicologist, polymath and premier social networker who lived in Lynn for nine years.

In 2001 the Rose and Crown pub closed leaving this busy and popular village with no public house, an increasingly common problem. In this case the Borough Council of King's Lynn and West Norfolk made a brave decision and bought the pub, negotiated with a local group of keen beer drinking activists, and now the Dabbling Duck is the popular restoration of a centuries' long tradition on the village scene.

RAF Massingham started as a satellite grass airfield to RAF West Raynham in 1940. Blenheim aircraft belonging to 2 Group Bomber Command played an important part in the Ruhr offensive. It was sold in 1958 and is now a private airfield. A Roll of Honour was dedicated in 1998 at a Memorial Service at St. Andrews Church, Little Massingham, listing all the crewmen and residents including details of operations and place of burial. Seven crewmen are buried in the graveyard.

Great Massingham

WEST NORFOLK

Castle Acre is one of the most interesting and attractive villages in Norfolk. It stands on the northern slope of the Nar valley in 'Norfolk's Holy Land' which abounded in religious houses. The estate was one of many granted to William de Warrenne by William the Conqueror. The Warrenne family firstly built an elaborate stone country house which was converted in the mid-12th century into one of the grandest motte-and-bailey castles in England controlling the Peddars Way and the Nar Valley; it was a powerful statement of Norman ambition. The whole of the early town was comfortably enfolded within a ditched and walled enclosure. Through the Bailey Gate, which arches over the road today, came Lord, knight, soldiers, artisans, workmen and country folk. Main Street is a diversion of the Peddars Way, and Pales Green was probably the original market of c. 1100.

The Cluniac Priory was built by William de Warrenne's son in about 1090. This was home to 30 monks and numerous lay people easily afforded by the very wealthy monastic order which became richer and richer through gifts and endowment of land. But this conspicuous consumption made them and other wealthy monasteries progressively less popular and, in reaction, Friaries were founded which renounced wealth and subsisted on charity. The Priory at Castle Acre continued to add to its buildings nevertheless, with a magnificent gateway about 1500 which now opens on to a sweep of lawns of 36 acres and a delightful Tudor house which was the Prior's lodging. English Heritage have the care of these partially ruined survivals.

The large St. James Church of about 1300 is situated between the outer castle bailey and the Priory. There is a side priests' doorway with a blocked up archway above which has given us the charming notion that mounted knights rode their horses into the church for blessing before battle.

Another nice little story concerns the fate of the village after the Reformation, when Lord Chief Justice Edward Coke, the ancestor of Lord Leicester, who is today the Lord of the Manor, approached Elizabeth I asking if he could buy more land. The Queen was determined that a subject should not have too much power and land so prevaricated until Coke said "just one more acre" of land would satisfy him. The Queen agreed. That acre was the village of Castle Acre.

Castle Acre

WEST NORFOLK

Alan Castleton

This fen-side village bursts with interest. It has a working corn windmill, a pleasant village centre around the carrstone church of St. Mary's, a famous person from a fine grand house, and the huge engineering works of the Denver Sluice.

Denver Hall has acclaim to both beauty and fame for in this fine old brick house with turrets, stepped gables, dormers, patterned chimneys and an exuberance of windows, was born Captain George Manby who invented the life-saving rocket apparatus in 1808 which could shoot a line from shore to stricken ship. Many sailors' lives were saved. His brother, Thomas, sailed around the world with Captain George Vancouver of Lynn.

Land and water are precariously balanced in this part of West Norfolk so the difference between fertility and flood may be mere inches. Since 1651 various Denver sluices and cuts have attempted the management of water from a large part of the fens. Now Denver Sluice and modern engineering have secured equilibrium for the present. Three huge structures, the Denver Sluice itself, the adjacent Navigation Lock and the A. P. Wright Sluice, perform the flood defence role of controlling the river waters. The lock is used for navigation between Denver and the Middle Level and also down the Tidal River to the Wash. Other locks and sluices are the Impounding Sluice, which sends water to Essex, the Residual Flow Sluice, which measures low flows of water during drought periods, the Diversion Sluice which has a drop leaf gate allowing water from the Ely Ouse to the Cut-off Channel and the Welmore Sluice which regulates water from the Ouse Washes. The technically minded could find a whole new interest in the many intakes, pumping stations, pipelines and outfalls which govern the water from Denver to Hanningfield Reservoir about 120 miles away on the Essex coast.

The windmill has been restored by a trust of local people, so on certain days the mill works, its sails turn, corn is ground and bread is baked. The mill is a fine sight rising across the flat lands above the surrounding buildings.

Denver Windmill

WEST NORFOLK

Alan Castleton

Downham Market is a self contained little town with a prosperous farming hinterland, good communications and infrastructure for light industry and engineering on an industrial estate about a mile from the town centre named the Trafalgar Industrial Estate and why not. Set on a fen island, it is a neat prosperous little town now bursting out of its ancient boundaries as housing estates burgeon on its outskirts. It is within easy commuter travel by train to Cambridge 'silicon fen' and it also attracts retiring couples from the more expensive south who want rural peace and quiet. Downham Market is situated on the road from Lynn to London with communication improved firstly by the Turnpike Trust road from Lynn which ended in Cannon Square where a stone marker reads *'End of Lynn Southgate Turnpike Trust'* and is one of 300 remaining markers in Norfolk. The first railway link from Lynn came to Downham in 1846, a distance of 11 miles travelled in 35 minutes.

Downham Market is easily recognised by its ornamental tower clock situated in the market place, and designed by William Cunliffe in a Gothic style and made of London cast iron. It is a gingerbread town of mellow carrstone with several rather nice buildings including the 19th century town hall. The 13th century carrstone church of St. Edmund overlooks the town with fine views over the fens from its high tower.

The River Great Ouse runs by its westward side where a thriving port existed to bring farmers' goods down inland waterways to market until the railway and the Relief Channel cut off its easy access to the town. The old name of Dunhamhithe indicates Downham Market's river port origins and in 1568 seventeen *'monstrous fysh'* were caught in the Ouse here each between 20 and 27 feet long.

The 1845 trade directory lists 8 pubs and two prosperous 17th century coaching houses, the Castle and the Crown. In 1807 Martin King, the boots at the Castle, a 'dwarf' under 4 feet, was found dead 'though excessive drink'. Both inns are still trading today and three pubs have survived.

One must briefly mention the supposed Nelson connection in Downham Market and be content to leave the veracity of his schooldays in this town to its local historians. But it is the case that Charles I stayed at the Swan Inn in April 1646 when escape abroad through Lynn was determined upon. Unfortunately parliamentary watches were kept on the river and no boat could be hired so the King and his two companions stayed at Snore Hall manor house at nearby Fordham until a treaty with the Scots was deemed the best course; it was not, he was betrayed; conviction and execution inevitable.

Downham Market

WEST NORFOLK

Alan Castleton.

Great works of engineering have been undertaken in the fens to improve the flow of water through the lower Ouse to the sea. One scheme was the Middle Level Drain completed in 1848, a completely new drain cut straight for ten miles taking water from the Middle Level to the lower junction with the Ouse at Wiggenhall St. Germans and relieving the traditional outlets at Salter's Lode and Tong's Drain. It involved building Norfolk's only aqueduct at Mullicourt Priory where it passes under the ancient Well Creek. The old river flowed in high banks kept moist and plump from its waters while the land around had shrunk dramatically, thus the new cut was engineered in much lower land. The success of fenland drainage, its problems, its effect on local topography and the ingenuity of man are succinctly and graphically demonstrated at the Mullicourt Priory site.

No sign now remains of Mullicourt Priory, which was dedicated to St. Mary Bello Loco, but it existed as a small Saxon monastery, though the date and founder are unknown. It was so poor a living with constant flooding that by the time of Henry VI (1445) only one lonely monk could be sustained there.

Alterations to the fenland rivers starved the Well Stream of water and this once mighty natural waterway, carrying water from the surrounding high ground, was unable to carry real commercial shipping after the 17th century. Coal for drainage pumps and sugar beet were still water borne, but by the 1970s no good reason to keep it could be seen by the Middle Level Drainage Board. An active group of protesters saved the Well Creek by forming the Well Creek Trust which aims to ensure the survival and enjoyment of this ancient river for all time.

The Well Creek is now a lovely tranquil river with leisure craft, fishing, walking and bird watching passing through the 'Wella' villages of Outwell, Upwell, Welney, Christchurch, Three Holes, Euximoor, Lakesend, Tipps End and Nordelph.

Well Creek

MULLICOURT AQUEDUCT, UPWELL

There are four Wiggenhalls a few miles south of King's Lynn which lie in fenland crossed by the Middle Level Drain, the Ouse and the Relief Channel. St. Germans is the largest named for Saint Germain who was Bishop of Paris c. 496-576 and, known as the 'Father of the Poor', he was canonised in 754 by Pope Stephen II. The other Wiggenhalls are St. Mary the Virgin, St. Mary Magdalen and St. Peter's, with its near perfect ruined church.

The rich fen soil specialises in growing vegetables. In 1895 Richard Allen of Wiggenhall St. Germans changed from growing corn, which could be imported cheaply from the vast American plains, to planting thousands of fruit trees and a large acreage of strawberries. In turn canning and jamming factories grew up on the outskirts of Lynn. Until the 1970s orchards of native apple trees abounded, then the French Delicious (so called) undercut the English apple market and acres were grubbed up.

Wiggenhall St. Germans had, for centuries, the nearest bridge to Lynn across the Ouse which gave, in 1310, the encroaching Lord of Castle Rising, Robert Montalt the chance to exhort heavy tolls from the traders crossing the bridge and power over those rowing and flowing on the river below. His agents intimidated and attacked boat and lighter users by dropping heavy stones and great lumps of earth onto them from the bridge until they paid up. Some river traders *being broken down and greatly impoverished* gave up, sold their boats and got a different job.

But later this same bridge was used for *'the common good'* in, for example, 1565 when a series of bad harvests led to near famine and the Bishop of Peterborough used the bridge to stop merchants shipping precious corn up to Lynn and thence abroad at great profit but depleting the local market. A massive increase in grain smuggling and the impoverishment of the simple porters and sailors of the port of Lynn who relied on foreign corn exports were, perhaps not considered, consequences.

There are two houses in the village worth noticing. A late 17th century hall, St. Germaine's, faces the River Ouse with a rare surviving contemporary gazebo in the garden, and Fitton Oake built in 1570 but, alas, alterations between 1976-1980 have virtually obliterated the exterior's Elizabethan appearance.

Wiggenhall St. Germans

WEST NORFOLK

Alan Castleton

The best symbol of marshland's medieval wealth is undoubtedly the architecture of its parish churches. Though often surrounded by very ordinary modern developments these churches are large, sumptuous and varied. The church of St. Clement is a cathedral-like masterpiece largely of the 15th century. Its north-west tower is 87 ft high and was a life saver in the 1670 floods when the whole village took refuge in the tower, and food was sent by boat from Lynn. Many of these marshland towns divided into smaller parishes as the population grew, so there are four Wiggenhalls and two Terringtons. St. John's started as a poor cousin to St. Clement but was rebuilt in 1423 and is now a fine church with a very pleasing, elegant tower. But despite these subdivisions making very small parishes, the value of the livings was prodigious. Terrington St. Clement was worth more than any other mentioned in the Ecclesiastical Taxation records of 1291.

A fine old house in the village is called Orange House. It was owned at one time by Hendrik, Baron Fagel (1765-1838), a Chief Minister in the Netherlands who fled to England at Napoleon's conquest and was visited by his friend Prince William of Orange. He renamed the house after his illustrious visitor. There is also an Orange Farm and Orange Row in the village.

Salt-making was a thriving industry around the Wash flourishing from the Iron Age until the 17th century. In the late 16th century Terrington St. Clement made one ton of salt each year. The spoil from the initial filtering of the brine before boiling was thrown onto heaps called salterns still distinguishable today in the local landscape. Other industries were farming, fishing and wildfowling.

Since Saxon times 25 square miles of land between the River Great Ouse and the River Nene have been claimed from the sea by embanking portions of marshland and gradually pushing the sea shore northwards. On this new land prosperous large farms and farmhouses were planted. Lord William Bentinck (1774-1839), the second son of the Duke of Portland, left India in 1807 and, with other members of the Bentinck family, established Bentinck, Pierrepoint, Rhoon and Welbeck Farms. This part of marshland is known as Governor Bentinck's Marsh.

In 1216 King John lost his treasure when the sea rushed across these marshes at each tide and his baggage train, which was on its way from Lynn to Newark, was overtaken and lost.

Terrington St. Clement

WEST NORFOLK

Alan Castleton

Palm Paper Limited took the decision to build a £400 million new paper mill at Lynn and production began in 2009 with a skilled workforce of 150. The town was favoured as a location because of the availability of a large riverside site adjacent to a power station. About 1000 tonnes of waste paper daily is transported to the plant from across East Anglia. At the same time 60 or more lorry loads of newsprint leave the paper mill on giant rolls each day to feed the presses of various newspaper groups.

The mill building is 500 metres long and pulp moves through the machinery at 75mph, being 99 percent water at the beginning and 92 percent paper at the end of the process. To ensure a correct water content is crucial. Heated rollers which dry the paper sometimes generate clouds of steam.

Dr Wolfgang Palm is the chief executive of the parent German paper company Papierfabrik Palm. He has remarked how, 50 years ago, recycled paper makers were machine operators but their jobs are now computerised, allowing workers to sit in a comfortable office. He decided to relocate to Lynn after meeting leaders and officers of the Borough Council. It is interesting to note that Lynn is the only English member of the New Hanseatic League of North European towns and was a partner of the German Hanse in the 14th and 15th centuries. Here is an example of modern Anglo-German cooperation.

Palm Paper overlooks the Eau Brink Cut which was excavated by 1000 navvies between 1818 and 1821 at a cost of £500,000 to bypass a giant loop in the Great Ouse between Lynn and St. Germans. As a result both navigation and drainage were improved. An Act of Parliament had been needed. At the public opening of the Cut, or canal, in July 1821 thousands thronged the banks to welcome a steam ship with a band on board and numerous pleasure craft. The latter entered the new river through the drawbridge integrated into the first bridge ever built across the Ouse at Lynn. Today's bridge is the fourth in this location and an essential road link between the town and the North.

As Palm Paper can be said to represent Lynn's 21st century industrial regeneration, so Campbell Soups UK was the harbinger for the town's 20th century industrial revolution. Built in 1958, the factory has recently closed, but its tower still stands as a symbol of that watershed in local history.

Palm Paper

KING'S LYNN

CAMPBELL'S TOWER

Alan Castleton

The most formidable structure in Lynn's medieval fortifications has miraculously survived when some other towns have lost all their ancient gates. The South Gate was rebuilt in brick and stone in the 1430s and 1440s, acquiring an ashlar front in 1520. Distinguished visitors to the town were offered refreshments in a large room on the upper floor. Pedestrian passages were driven through the building in the 1840s. It was restored by the Borough Council in the 1980s but increasingly heavy traffic passes under its arch. Public access to this fascinating historic monument is possible thanks to a volunteer group who open it in the summer.

Not only did the South Gate have a drawbridge and portcullis as well as gun ports to greet the traveller but, until 1741, an armed custodian to apprehend 'vagabonds' and tax road traffic on behalf of the Mayor. Plague victims were forced to live outside the town's gates in the 16th and 17th centuries in temporary booths. Public executions were moreover staged outside the South Gate and perhaps the most gruesome in 1708 when the young Michael and Ann Hamond were hanged for theft.

People and wagons arriving at the South Gate turned sharp left to reach the town centre via Friar Street until the construction of London Road (1803-06). This  was Lynn's first bypass! The population of South Lynn between the South Gate and the Millfleet climbed from 701 to 4772 in the 50 years after 1801 with London Road its principal thoroughfare. Proud citizens saw it as a new approach to Lynn equal to that of any other town with its 'handsome' and 'elegant' houses built in the course of the 19th century. Road traffic into Lynn no longer passes through the ancient heart of South Lynn where All Saints' stands just off Friar Street. Its main treasure is an anchorite's cell which projects from the south side of the chancel and was probably a late 14th century addition. A succession of anchoresses lived in this little house and chapel like Katherine Sampson in 1408.

The South Gate was built beside a fosse close to the Nar and its roof provided a spectacular grandstand for civic worthies to view ship launches on the river. Lynn railway worker Edward Dow wrote in his notebook for 4th October 1853: '*This day about 7am a barque was launched by the South Gate*' and '*there were about three thousand persons present upon the banks of the river and other places*' whilst '*a band of music was in attendance and guns firing during the proceedings*'. Considerable civic pride is evident in these festivities but Lynn's shipbuilding industry was soon to end unable to compete with the yards of northern ports such as Newcastle and Sunderland.

The South Gate

AND LONDON ROAD, KING'S LYNN

ALL SAINTS' CHURCH

Alan Castleton

The industrial towns of Victorian England created parks for the recreation of their inhabitants but Lynn's great park has its origins in Georgian urban improvement. A large part of the green belt between the medieval defences and the built-up area was landscaped in the 1750s by the town's merchant rulers. Running through it was a Mall or Walk 340 yards long for *the accommodation of the public at large'* though it was for the pleasure of the rich rather than the poor. At the eastern end of the Walk is the North Guanock Gate, once part of the town fortifications, but rebuilt as a *'picturesque'* local feature about 1800.

On a small hill nearby is the Red Mount Chapel recently repaired by the Borough Council with the help of the Heritage Lottery Fund. The latter made a substantial grant to allow the restoration of the Walks as one of England's most attractive urban parks. Pevsner described the Red Mount in 1961 as *'one of the strangest Gothic Churches in England.'* Built as a wayside Chapel for pilgrims en route from Lynn to the Shrine of Our Lady at Walsingham in North Norfolk, it was on the outside edge of Lynn's medieval defences. Of red brick and octagonal, the Chapel was closed in the 1530s when pilgrimages were *'forbyden'.* The cruciform stone chapel on the top of the building was added in 1506 and has a fine vault attributed to John Wastell who worked on King's College Chapel in Cambridge. It was used as reservoir (lower chapel), Civil War fort, navigation school and stable.

The Walks were extended beyond the North Guanock Gate in the 19th and 20th centuries for townspeople to enjoy sport and recreation. A marshy meadow was converted into a recreation ground in 1902 offering *'another source of pleasure and improvement to the welfare of the population'.* A bandstand and a swimming pool were built as well as a football stadium for the 'Linnets'. Perhaps the most dramatic event staged in The Walks in the 20th century was the 1954 Town Pageant which celebrated the 750th anniversary of Lynn's first royal charter of borough freedom.

The Guanock Gate and Red Mount Chapel

KING'S LYNN

Alan Castleton

The Saturday Market Place was the location of both the ecclesiastical and secular authorities of Bishop's Lynn embodied in St. Margaret's Priory Church and the Holy Trinity Guildhall respectively. The latter was the headquarters of the town's merchant rulers who eroded the local power of the Norwich bishops through the acquisition of royal charters. Today's edifice, with its distinctive south gable of flint and limestone in a chequer pattern, masks a brick building of the 1420s. The hall is on the first floor and the undercroft below stored valuable goods before becoming a prison in 1571 and now houses Lynn's magnificent regalia. The porch to the left of the Hall was erected in 1624 in the classical style. In the 18th century the Mayor proclaimed war and peace on these steps as Britain fought Spain and France for world supremacy.

Behind the Trinity Guildhall are the assembly rooms constructed of Ely brick in 1767 for £1300 to facilitate gatherings of merchants and the landed aristocracy of the region. The making of the Mayor every September was the grandest of these 'Lynn feasts'. Nelson, Vancouver, George III and Robert Walpole are amongst the impressive portraits looking down on the mayoral receptions, concerts and Council meetings of modern times. The morning Coffee Concerts are an important part of the musical programme of the King's Lynn Festival every July.

GREYFRIARS TOWER

The Town Hall comprises the medieval Guildhall, Georgian assembly rooms and Victorian council chamber and, all together, it never fails to inspire visitors. Next door stands the Old Gaol House which today accommodates an exhibition on Lynn's macabre story of crime and punishment. Of white brick and classical features, the building cost £450 in 1784. In 1814 mariners attempted to release their strike leaders from the prison but were stopped by Mayor Self who declared that no person would break through the doors *except through the body of the mayor'*. There was a whipping post in the market place last used in 1847. There is still a Saturday market but its extent is unfortunately rather less than in the past when stalls hugged the surrounding buildings and ran into High Street.

From the Saturday Market Place can be seen the brick and stone tower of the Franciscan church at Lynn erected about 1400 and escaping destruction during the Henrician Reformation of the 1530s and 1540s because of its usefulness as a seamark. Amazingly it remains a dominant feature of the townscape of the Wash port after 600 years.

Holy Trinity Guildhall

AND TOWN HALL, KING'S LYNN

Alan Castleton

The twin towers of St. Margaret's are Lynn's most striking architectural feature and dominant in that panorama of the town from the west which the artist Walter Dexter found so *'arresting'* and *'exceptional'*. This Priory Church was founded by Bishop Losinga of Norwich about 1100.

It was rebuilt on a grander scale in the early 13th century and both towers had taken today's form by the 1450s when the north-west one had to be reconstructed. A central lantern similar to that on Ely cathedral and a new spire on the south-west tower were added in the 1480s. When Oliver Cromwell's army was bombarding Lynn from West Lynn in 1643, a cannon ball passed through the west window and caused havoc but hurt nobody. The tall spire was thrown into the nave by a violent storm in September 1741 and this part of St. Margaret's was rebuilt on a smaller scale.

St. Margaret's was first erected by the waterside but silting and rubbish dumping by the urban population caused the river bank to move westwards. In the 1580s a large brick and stone warehouse was constructed abutting on the Ouse due west of the Church, probably the work of the Clayborne family who traded in salt and corn. A town map of 1830 still has the building against the river but one in 1846 shows a new bank had appeared due to silting. Soon railway lines were laid allowing wagons to access what became the new South Quay.

The Millennium Project undertaken by the Borough Council in the 1990s involved the enhancement of the South Quay and the restoration of the Tudor warehouse to accommodate the Green Quay. The latter is a tourist attraction and education centre as well as a community facility run by an independent trust and opened in May 2000. Just to the south is the Hanse House restored for offices by Norfolk County Council in 1971. This former commercial complex was built around a courtyard about 1480 by the Hanseatic League, the original premises granted by Edward IV in 1475. The property remained in German hands until 1751 when sold to a Lynn merchant who rebuilt the street range facing St. Margaret's. Called St. Margaret's House during the 20th century, this Grade One listed building was renamed Hanse House in 2009 as England's sole Hanseatic medieval trading post.

St. Margaret's

KING'S LYNN FROM THE WEST

Alan Castleton

Probably Lynn's most famous landmark is the Custom House designed by Henry Bell for John Turner. It was opened in 1685 as an Exchange for merchants. Of Ketton stone, this distinctive classical building marked a turning point in town architecture, and is recognised as a brilliant example of England's urban renaissance after 1660. For Pevsner the Custom House is *'one of the finest late 17th century public buildings in provincial England'* standing on the Purfleet *'in a most becoming situation'.*

The Crown purchased the Exchange to serve solely as a Custom House in 1717 when Lynn was still amongst England's premier ports. Foreign trade revenues at the Custom House were *'exceeded'* by few ports in *'the kingdom',* the Corporation was informed by George II's government in 1743. Ceres and Bacchus are represented on the west elevation, telling us that corn and wine were the commodities which enriched Lynn's merchants. Spacious cellars can be found on both sides of the Purfleet where cranes were erected to load and unload ships. A new one was built in 1719 for example. Due west of the Custom House is the statue of Lynn's George Vancouver (1757-1798) who explored the west coast of North America for the British Admiralty in his ship *The Discovery.*

The Custom House was sold by the British government in 1989 to a property developer before the Borough Council secured a long lease on this classical gem. It was opened by

CLIFTON HOUSE PORCH

HRH Prince Charles in March 1999 as a Tourist Information Centre complemented by displays on Lynn's maritime heritage on the first floor. By March 2009 over 900,000 people had visited the Custom House thus demonstrating public access to the town's most iconic building has been achieved.

On the south bank of the Purfleet is King's Staithe Square where traders in corn and wine resorted in the late summers of Georgian Lynn to bargain. Today this attractive urban space has a platform, or stage, built into the flood defences for public concerts or performances. Adjacent is Bank House built on the riverbank in the early 18th century and remodelled in the 1780s when it became the Lynn Bank. Its classical front is enhanced by a statue of James I brought from another site about 1703. This merchant mansion is now a hotel and restaurant.

The wealthiest merchants of Lynn were vintners and Clifton House in nearby Queen Street was remodelled by the Taylor family about 1700 with its main entrance adorned by baroque 'barley sugar' columns. The tower built onto this grand mansion by George Walden in the 1570s overlooks King's Staithe Square.

The Custom House

KING'S LYNN

Alan Castleton

King Street is Lynn's grandest historic street but began as a river bank with the first merchants' houses on the east side, though little remains of the earliest buildings here. The exception is the timber-framed 28-32 King Street where the gable ends of a stone house erected about 1180 can be found. By 1350 merchants began to develop domestic and commercial complexes on the west side of the street, the Ouse moving westwards through rubbish dumping and silting. Apart from St. George's Guildhall, no other medieval building now stands intact because of extensive remodelling, especially in the 18th century.

For Pevsner King Street is *the richest in pleasant houses*. Red or yellow brick elevations of the 18th century predominate but numbers 15A and 27 are cased in limestone to flaunt the wealth of the owners. St. George's Chambers (no. 27) is probably the finest mansion in the street matching some of the best Georgian houses in Bath. It was sold by Hannah Flierden to Benjamin Nuthall for £1390 in 1762. These homes of Lynn's merchant princes of the past have been converted to accommodate accountants, solicitors and dentists.

Due to war time destruction in London and York, St. George's Guildhall is the largest medieval guild premises in England but it was due for demolition in 1945 for a garage. Alexander Penrose purchased it. Public grants and an appeal fund led to the restoration of this magnificent Hall

MAJESTIC CINEMA

by 1951, with Lord and Lady Fermoy playing key roles, and HM Queen Elizabeth giving her support. The first King's Lynn Festival of Music and the Arts in July 1951 was organised to celebrate the rescue of St. George's Guildhall which is its artistic and architectural heart. The 60th anniversary of this annual prestigious event was marked in July 2010.

Plays were almost certainly performed in St. George's Guildhall from the 1440s so few English public buildings can claim such a long association with the drama. The Georgian theatre built inside the ancient Hall in 1766 closed in 1814 and the property became a warehouse. The undercroft was let to wine and spirit merchants as well as becoming a depository for ice blocks from Norway for sale to fishmongers amongst others. Lynn scenic artist G. M. Bridges & Son occupied St. George's Guildhall in the 1920s and 1930s and won international fame for their work. Cultural change shaped by the cinema was to signal the demise of firms of scenic artists who had depended on music halls, theatres, funfairs and exhibitions. In 1928 the Majestic opened in Tower Street, being proclaimed as *the last word in luxurious picture theatre* in the eastern counties and *as good as any in London*. St. George's Guildhall has also served as a town cinema for many years as well as a theatre and concert venue.

King Street

AND ST. GEORGE'S GUILDHALL, KING'S LYNN

Alan Castleton

The Culley farming brothers from Northumberland visited Lynn in 1784. They were impressed with the market place which was *'a fine square'* and, on the north side, *'the cross and shambles'* formed a crescent with poultry, butter and eggs in rows and livestock behind. They were astonished by the big business in barley and wheat transacted here on Tuesdays as farmers brought their samples in paper bags for inspection by merchants. There was no market hall to accommodate them until 1830 and this was replaced in 1854 by a larger Corn Exchange with its *'jolly and vulgar'* classical stone façade topped by the Goddess of Corn. It opened in 1855 and cost £3000. With the decline of Lynn's corn market this spacious hall was booked for a variety of public purposes, including pop concerts in the 1960s, but it remained underused and uncomfortable.

The Corn Exchange was extended and remodelled in the 1990s by the Borough Council which secured 50 percent of the £4.6 million expenditure from The National Lottery. It has become a popular town theatre and concert hall with its original and bold façade still overlooking the market place. Every summer top British and European orchestras play to packed houses during the King's Lynn Festival of Music and the Arts.

The Tuesday Market Place had been transformed in the 18th century as new brick fronts in classical style masked older properties and this is particularly evident on the north side. Here can be found the witch's heart carved on the upper floor of numbers 14-16 whose smart new façade of the 1720s pulled together several late medieval houses. The Bagge family rebuilt Bishop's Lynn house in the 1720s and the northern part in 1803-04 behind which maltings and warehouses ran down to the Ouse. A grand classical mansion was erected by George Hogge in 1768. It was amongst the buildings admired by the French aristocrat de la Rochefoecald in 1784: *'The market square is large and handsome and there are some fine buildings looking onto it, among them Mr Hogge's house, which is certainly a large and beautiful building'*. The latter is now Barclays Bank. Elsewhere around this exceptional urban space can be found more banks, estate agents, lawyers, dentists and restaurants. The Tuesday market itself still attracts town and country folk but its size has diminished since the 1970s.

Since the 1950s the Tuesday Market Place has unhappily functioned as a car park for most days in the year. The weekly Tuesday and Friday markets and February Mart help to retain its traditional colour and character. So, in addition, does Festival Too whose programme of popular music draws thousands to the square for two weeks every summer and celebrated its 25th anniversary in 2010.

Tuesday Market Place

KING'S LYNN

The Duke's Head was designed by Henry Bell for John Turner who wanted to attract more foreign merchants to Lynn, and this imposing coaching inn opened in 1686. It is a distinctive classical building whose red brick was plastered over about 1800. Unfortunately, a plain and uninspiring brick extension in 1967 resulted in a loss of some historical features. Stage coaches entered through the main doors into a courtyard overlooked by wooden galleries giving access to the oak panelled rooms. There were parlours and a dining room with a music gallery as well as a cock room 'for fighting cocks'. Ship auctions were also held and in 1774 William Bagge bought the brig *William and Mary* of 140 tons for £300. *The Sun* coach left the Duke's Head for London three times a week in 1793 when the 100 mile journey cost indoor passengers 25 shillings.

The Duke's Head was a high status venue where Lynn's upper crust made merry at various events in the annual social calendar. Sir Robert Walpole was one of the town's two members in 17 parliaments between 1702 and 1742 with the victory parties organised here. In 1721 the landlord advertised an assembly for gentlefolk to coincide with Lynn's February Mart, a commercial and pleasure fair catering for all social classes. The Mayor and Corporation processed through the streets to the Tuesday Market Place preceded by 'music and drums' to open it. Yet by the 1840s the Lynn Mart was in decline as improved communications rendered such annual fairs unnecessary and, by the 1880s, it had been transformed by the steam-driven roundabouts of Frederick Savage. He won international fame as the pioneer of the modern funfair and Lynn Mart renown in turn. It is still opened every 14th February by the Borough Mayor followed by a traditional civic luncheon at the Town Hall attended by members of the Showmen's Guild of Great Britain.

Celebrations of all kinds have taken place in the Tuesday Market Place. One of the greatest was the Peace Festival on 22nd July 1814 when over 6,000 townspeople sat down for a dinner provided by Lynn's merchant families to signal the return of peace after the victory over Napoleon. In July 1821 the bells of St. Margaret's peeled out as country people poured into town to mark the coronation of George IV. Whilst 200 of Lynn's 'high caste folk' dined at the Trinity Guildhall the populace was treated to a roast bullock and strong ale followed by fireworks on the Tuesday Market Place. It was however also the town arena for public executions like that of Mary Taylor burnt at the stake in 1730 for being an accomplice in the murder of her mistress.

Tuesday Market Place 2

KING'S LYNN

Alan Castleton

To regenerate the Port of Lynn the Alexandra and Bentinck docks were constructed in 1869 and 1883 respectively with ships accessing both via the Estuary Cut excavated in 1850-53. Victorian warehouses were demolished in the later 20th century for modern sheds but 15 silos were built in 2000 with a total capacity of 25,000 tonnes of foodstuffs. It is remarkable to what extent wheat and barley remain crucial to the buoyancy of the Port of Lynn and, in turn, the annual yield of the East Anglian harvest. Corn has been its principal export since the 16th century.

Timber is a significant import as it has been for 700 years. Fertiliser, rapeseed, scrap, maize, malt and beans were other cargoes carried by vessels using Lynn docks in 2009. The riverside quay adjacent to the dock gates was constructed in 1990 to handle ships of 5,000 tonnes dead weight or the total tonnage of everything a vessel carries.

Just to the south of the docks is the Common Staith. Though today it is yet another town car park, for about 400 years before 1869 it was Lynn's most important public quay. In 1737 Mackerell emphasised the significance of Common Staith Yard where there was 'a large crane to take up heavy goods from the key'. Common Staith is also the home of the Conservancy Board occupying the Victorian

LYNN FERRY

swimming baths and pilot tower. In 1889 a steamer from Baltimore carrying maize ran aground in the channel to the Port of Lynn and obstructed sea traffic, involving the Corporation in a hugely expensive operation to remove the wreck. An Act of Parliament set up the Conservancy Board in 1898 to safeguard the channel by maintaining navigational aids and pilotage services.

The Lynn ferry links West Lynn with the town centre for commuters and shoppers. In the 15th century there were two ferries managed by the Holy Trinity Guild to avoid the long detour into Lynn via St. Germans up river. Tragedies occurred. In 1796 the ferry with 20 passengers sank with 11 lives lost including a young couple found *clasped in each other's arms*. Rowing boats were used until 1920 when two petrol driven craft were introduced.

King's Lynn Docks

AND THE RIVER

AlanCastleton

St. Nicholas, the patron saint of sailors and merchants, gave his name to this Chapel-of-Ease to St. Margaret's, founded in 1146, and rebuilt about 1200 as Lynn expanded. A tower was soon added. The present and much larger Chapel was constructed in the early 15th century in perpendicular style and completed by 1419. Though other parts of St. Nicholas are in stone, beside the tower and south porch, brick was used extensively for the building. It is perhaps the best example in Norfolk of the influence of the friars who erected large preaching churches for urban congregations.

With its great east and west windows as well as ingenious west front St. Nicholas was designed to impress and probably rival St. Margaret's. The outstanding skill of the master carpenter is demonstrated by the installation of the first angel roof after London's Westminster Hall. The fine merchant memorials from the 17th and 18th centuries make the interior even more interesting and remarkable. During the great storm of 8th September 1741 the spire on St. Margaret's crashed into the nave but that on the Chapel fortunately fell into the graveyard. It had provided an important seamark for shipping approaching Lynn and a replacement was quickly raised until removal in 1854. Today's *pretty* lead spire by Gilbert Scott was made in 1869 following local fund raising.

FISHING NETS

In the late 19th century St. Nicholas was attracting fisherfolk from the surrounding yards and streets of the North End where Primitive Methodism had been influential in the 1820s and 1830s. This traditional and close knit community was broken up by *the slum clearances* of the 1930s and demolition for road widening in the 1960s. A row of houses in Pilot Street has fortunately been preserved immediately to the east of the Chapel. The sole fisherfolk yard with cottages to have survived redevelopment is the central feature of the nearby True's Yard Museum, founded by volunteers in 1991. It was enlarged in 2009 by the integration of two more cottages in St. Ann's Street and Lynn's last smokehouse restored on the premises, largely through a grant from the Heritage Lottery Fund. HM The Queen, accompanied by HRH Prince Philip, opened the extension in February 2010. This fascinating museum and heritage site is an education and community centre as well as a tourist destination.

St. Nicholas Chapel

AND THE NORTH END, KING'S LYNN

The Lynn and Ely Railway Company purchased land for £25,000 for the town's first railway station erected in wood by John Sugars in 1846. Its location on Blackfriars Road involved the removal of what was left of the Dominican friary and part of the medieval town wall; at the same time it inevitably encouraged the building of new streets in the vicinity. Not thought to be grand enough for such an ancient borough, the railway station was rebuilt of brick in a *'vaguely classical'* style in 1872.

Lynn had become a railway town by 1914 with another station at South Lynn due to its geographical position linking East Anglia with the North and Midlands, but Beeching's axe in the 1960s left only the line to London. Even this was in danger of being lost until the Borough Council intervened in 1989 to ensure that the electrification of the London track did not stop at Ely 30 miles to the south. Trains run frequently from Lynn to London taking approximately 100 minutes to reach King's Cross 100 miles away.

Lynn's railway connection to London was built by 1848 and cheap excursions to the capital allowed townspeople to visit the Great Exhibitions of 1851 and 1862. Just as dramatic was the opening of the line to New Hunstanton in 1862 which offered citizens excursions to the seaside resort just 16 miles to the north. That the railway could bring tears as well as joy was demonstrated in August 1863 when a train packed with day trippers approaching Lynn from Hunstanton was derailed by a bull on the line. This was the first East Anglian railway disaster and shocked Lynn's inhabitants who mourned eight dead and cared for 50 injured.

The purchase of Sandringham by the Royal family in 1861 excited townspeople who saw it as a good omen as Lynn's maritime economy was being undermined by railway competition. The Prince of Wales (the future Edward VII) and Princess Alexandra were married at Windsor in March 1863 and soon departed for Norfolk to rebuild their new home. The Royal train from London to Lynn was pulled by an engine painted white and profusely decorated with flowers.

Railway Station

KING'S LYNN

AlanCastleton

Bishop's Terrace is located roughly at the centre of Gaywood village and built in brick about 1600 as a single house with a symmetrical front. The ground floor has been much altered to accommodate shops. Its name recalls the fact the Gaywood was once in the hands of the Norwich bishops who erected a palace not far from here in the early 13th century. The lin, or estuarine lake, was simply the western seashore of their Gaywood estate on higher land to the east. When Bishop Losinga founded St. Margaret's Church about 1100 to help establish Lynn as a market town he was in effect sanctioning a second parish church to St. Faith's at Gaywood, but one serving a growing community some distance from the latter. Gaywood Hall was the home of the Bagge family until 1935 ('the squires' of Gaywood) and replaced an earlier house in 1851 on the site of the Bishop's Palace.

Bishop's Terrace overlooks the old Norwich Road which ran west from Gayton through Gaywood to Bishop's Lynn where the East Gate marked the medieval defences. Pilgrims from other parts of Britain and northern Europe, disembarking at Lynn in the 15th century, walked the 23 miles north-east to The Shrine of Our Lady at Walsingham. This Walsingham Way passed through Gaywood and along what is now Wootton and Grimston Roads towards North Norfolk.

Ribbon housing development had linked Lynn and Gaywood before 1914 and in 1935 the two were officially united with the Norfolk village becoming a suburb of the Borough of King's Lynn. Lynn had once been a suburb of Gaywood! Its population climbed sharply after the Bagge family sold their Gaywood estate to the Borough Council for the development of a housing estate. In 1962 Lynn signed an overspill agreement with London County Council and another large housing estate was built at Fairstead off Gayton Road. There had been a horse fair here every October in the 18th and 19th centuries as the name tells. Today Gaywood is by far the most populous of the Lynn parishes (about 20,000 residents) with its own shopping centre and the location of all three of the town's high schools.

The Memorial Clock stands in front of Bishop's Terrace after being moved from the centre of the road junction a little to the east and set on a plinth of engineering bricks. It is mainly of carrstone, probably from the quarry at nearby Snettisham, with a limestone base and dressings. The Memorial Clock was erected in 1920 in honour of the Gaywood men who fell during the Great War.

Gaywood

KING'S LYNN

78

The Origins of Lynn

Bishop's Lynn

In the course of the 11th century growing numbers of seaborne traders brought furs, cloth, millstones and other commodities into the lin, or estuarine lake, at the south-eastern corner of the Wash. Salt produced from the evaporation of sea water boiled in pans over peat fires was the major attraction, being in great demand to preserve foodstuffs. Sand was heaped into big containers and sea water channelled through them to pick up more salt before the boiling began. Waste discarded from these salt works raised the level of the land, pushing the high tide mark towards the sea thus shrinking the lin, of which nothing now remains.

Lynn in the 11th century was a harbour market with European and British merchants arriving by sea in the summer and pitching tents. On the sandy shores of the Wash they traded in salt and wool with the dealers who were also temporary residents from the locality and interior of East Anglia. The Domesday Book of 1086 tells us that Lynn had a very small permanent population and that the salt industry had been significant well before the Norman Conquest.

In the century or more following the Domesday Survey ordered by King William, this tiny Wash settlement was transformed as Europe's economy and population expanded. By the early 13th century Lynn (as in local parlance) had become a significant market town and seaport having grown rapidly since 1101 when Bishop Losinga of Norwich recognised it as a hamlet between the Millfleet and Purfleet on his Gaywood estate. He endowed the Benedictine monks of Norwich cathedral with the lordship. Their Priory Church of St. Margaret was, however, only to be built and rebuilt through the wealth of Lynn's mercantile community, though the Norwich bishops were determined to retain their grip on the town. They had founded a second town and market in the 1140s on the Newland to the north of the first and assumed the lordship of both centres, of Bishop's Lynn, in 1205. When Lynn received its first royal charter of borough freedom in 1204, giving its merchants a degree of self-government, it was already the fourth port of the Kingdom and a dynamic frontier town.

There was also an earlier settlement and parish church at South Lynn to the south of the Millfleet and beyond the jurisdiction of the Norwich bishops, but it grew far more slowly than Bishop's Lynn, though the town defences erected from the 12th century encompassed both. The South Gate, rebuilt in brick in the 15th century, is still an imposing structure for those approaching it. All Saints' at South Lynn can be said to be the town's oldest church. The rapid development of Bishop's Lynn led to the foundation of two Chapels-of-Ease to St. Margaret's; St. James (1130) and St. Nicholas (1146), and the friars were established in the Wash port before 1300. Dominicans, Franciscans, Augustinians and Carmelites all drew the patronage of local landed and merchant families. Recent archaeological work has established the full extent of the former house of the Franciscans whose church tower has recently been repaired by the Borough Council assisted by the Heritage Lottery Fund. The major archaeological survey of Lynn in the 1960s revealed much about the topography of the medieval town and confirmed that the river bank had moved west through silting and rubbish dumping.

Lynn's prominence in the Middle Ages depended on an extensive hinterland captured by the River Great Ouse and its tributaries, including several counties at the heart of the nation (the great river had been diverted from Wisbech to Lynn about 1270). This privileged geographical position was reinforced by its location on England's east coast, facing Europe across the North Sea, and London and Scotland within easy reach by ship, too. That Hanseatic merchants from Northern Germany were resident in the town in the 14th and 15th centuries testifies to its importance. Herring, timber, wax, furs, iron and pitch were imported into England via Lynn in their ships. Wool, skins, salt, lead and especially cloth were exported to Baltic harbours by Lynn and Hanseatic vessels. Lynn's wool and corn exports paid for the import of large quantities of wine from the vineyards of south-western France in the 13th and 14th centuries. Its merchants amassed fortunes as leading players in England's overseas commerce.

Lynn merchants in the 1330s and 1340s included men such as Robert Braunche who was courted by Edward III because of his economic prowess. The Braunche brass in St. Margaret's Church depicts a peacock feast at which the King was supposedly present. Thomas and William Melchebourne travelled to Lynn in the first decade of the 14th century from Bedfordshire and soon became prominent in the Wash port. Thomas built up a fleet of ships importing wine from France and fish from Norway whilst exporting wool, hides, grain, ale and cloth. Edward III employed him in the royal service. In 1343 Thomas reached the peak of his career when elected as head of the English Wool Company which took over the farming of the customs of the whole realm. Two years later however, the Melchebournes found themselves in serious financial difficulties in common with most English wool merchants. In 1337 they had built a galley called *La Philipe* of 60 or more oars for Edward III and probably one of the largest ships of its kind yet constructed. Thomas and William were also successively deputy royal butlers to collect taxes due to the King on wine imported into Lynn.

Lynn's population must have been about 10,000 on the eve of the Black Death in 1348 which confirms it was in the premier league of English towns. But this Great Pestilence of 1348/49 was equivalent to the impact of a nuclear war in the number of dead. Probably fifty percent of England's 5 million inhabitants perished. East Anglian towns like Lynn particularly suffered and outbreaks of the plague continued; however, economic and social recovery was marked. Neighbourhood guilds played a key role in knitting together damaged communities and a large part of the adult population was enrolled at Lynn. No less than 59 responded to a royal survey of English guilds in 1388.

Lynn's Borough Archive is accommodated in the Holy Trinity Guildhall and is of national importance because of its rich collection of medieval documents, including the town's royal charters from 1204. Facsimiles are on display in the Regalia Rooms where the King John Cup is exhibited. This unique and internationally famous silver gilt cup depicts men and women wearing the costumes of the 1330s and 1340s so can not have been made in the time of this King. It was, without doubt, in the possession of the Great Guild established in 1204 whose members regarded King John as their founder. Was the King John Cup adopted as a Founder's Cup? How it came to Lynn remains a puzzle. King John's prominent part in the early history of the town is portrayed on the west window of St. Margaret's Church. His last fateful journey started from Lynn in October 1216 when chroniclers tell us that the baggage train with his treasure was *'lost in the Wash'*. A dejected and unwell monarch continued north via Wisbech, only to die at Newark.

Wealth generated by home and foreign trade was invested by Lynn's medieval and later merchants in building projects of all kinds – ecclesiastical, civic, commercial and domestic. To walk from the Millfleet northwards to the Purfleet and on to True's Yard Fisherfolk Museum through the riverside streets must be one of the finest trails in England for historical and architectural interest. The report on Lynn by the Society for the Protection of Ancient Buildings in 1945 observed:

> *'The Halls of the Guilds and the magnitude of the Churches express the dignity of commerce no less than the public spirit of the citizens, and the merchant houses and capacious warehouses of the past bear witness to the long standing maritime importance of Lynn'.*

KING'S LYNN

In 1537 Bishop's Lynn became King's Lynn when the charter of Henry VIII finally dispossessed the Norwich bishops and transferred full political power to the town's merchants. The physical appearance of the Wash port was profoundly changed by the Reformation of the 1530s and 1540s because its friaries and other religious houses were completely or partially demolished. Today's tall Greyfriars tower survived due to its usefulness as a seamark. Houses and warehouses built or rebuilt in Tudor and Stuart Lynn were increasingly of brick rather than timber and rubble to alter

further the town's look. Its population in 1600 was probably about 6,000. For Alderman John Spence who was the owner of The Bull in High Street in 1610 Lynn was *'a large and populous towne and there is a great resorte of people there both by sea and by land'*. Migration from the rural hinterland helped to replenish such urban societies often devastated by the plagues during the 16th and 17th centuries.

Rising coal imports from the North-East by the 1560s reflect a period of English economic expansion and only London received more colliers than Lynn from England's 'Black Indies'. In exchange the Norfolk port shipped corn and other foodstuffs northwards and southwards to Newcastle and London respectively as this lucrative coastal trade kept its commercial wheels turning. Its prosperity between 1560 and 1700 is confirmed by the building and rebuilding in brick of warehouses and granaries in the riverside streets. During these Tudor and Stuart years Lynn also sent ships to Icelandic waters for cod and in 1614 Tobias Gentleman talked of the Wash port as *'a proper gallant town for seafaring men'* and *'of men of Iceland'*. Its merchants did not equip whaling ships for annual voyages to Greenland until the late 18th century when five or six vessels were employed.

Lynn's international trade with the Baltic and south-west France in timber and wine respectively continued in the 18th century and the coastal trade in coal and corn thrived.

Its hinterland remained the key to success. In 1722 the travel writer Daniel Defoe was impressed by the fact that the Wash haven enjoyed *the greatest extent* of inland navigation of any port outside London and served six counties *wholly* and three *in part* with coal, wine and provisions. The Norfolk port had moreover become a major corn exporter to Europe by the 1720s as its numerous granaries and maltings indicated. An educated traveller through East Anglia in 1741 thought that Lynn was *a tolerable good town* with a *very fine spacious* market place encompassed by *very decent buildings*. The people were *pretty rich* being *chiefly wine and coal merchants*. He identified probably the biggest local brewer: *Over against St. Nicholas's church is a pretty regular fronted house belonging to Mr Allen a brewer*. As important as brewing to the town's economy was shipbuilding, with local merchants commissioning vessels in yards at South Lynn and North End for their own fleets.

English provincial towns again changed character from the late 17th century by the adoption of classical architecture and improvements to the urban landscape. Lynn was no exception. The Exchange, or meeting place, for merchants (later the Custom House) of 1685 was the first town building *to use the grammar of classical architectural correctly*. Designed by the gifted part-time architect Henry Bell for the powerful Turner family, the Duke's Head coaching inn and a new Market Cross were also projects led by the same partnership. Bell was involved too in the building or re-modelling of grand mansions with Clifton House in Queen Street (1708) probably his work. Other merchant houses were built or rebuilt in brick in the classical style during the 18th century as the town walk which so delighted Sir John Betjeman in the 1950s affirms. Such high status properties ran back with yards and warehouses to the Great Ouse to contrast with the taverns and humble dwellings on the east side of these same riverside streets. Mackerell called Lynn *beautiful* and *large* in 1737 with *about 2360 houses* divided by four small rivers which had *about fifteen* bridges over them. With over 10,000 inhabitants in 1801 the town was about the same size as Ipswich.

Lynn's population doubled between 1801 and 1851 as East Anglian ports boomed by sending ships to feed London and the growing industrial regions. Then the coming of the railways in the 1840s robbed Lynn of its geographical advantages with river and coastal traffic giving way to the iron road. Population fell from 20,000 to 16,000 (1851-1871). These mid-Victorian years were, however, prosperous for regional farmers as England's urban population continued to rise and Lynn benefited through its role as an important market town. The big and bold Corn Exchange, opened on the Tuesday Market Place in 1855, testifies to this golden age for agriculture.

The Port of Lynn was rescued from long term decline by river improvement and two docks (1869 and 1883) connected to the national railway network. Now Lynn could export coal from the midland collieries to Europe and import more timber for the home construction industry as well as American corn. Flour and animal feed mills were set up by the waterside. Close to the docks Frederick Savage erected his St. Nicholas Ironworks in 1873, making steam traction engines and agricultural machinery and later the fairground roundabouts which earned him international fame. Artificial fertilisers were manufactured at the Muck Works in South Lynn where a second railway station was built (1862). The latter influenced the location in 1894 of the agricultural engineering factory of Thomas Cooper. A new Technical School to serve local industrial enterprises demonstrated that Lynn was investing in the future. Thus its first industrial revolution created a new society as the town's population began to grow again with suburban housing breaking through the medieval defences by 1900. At the Kettle Mills (formerly the town waterworks) Lynn's electricity station to light the borough opened in 1898.

By 1914 Lynn had been transformed in less than 50 years by an industrial revolution embodied in big factories on the northern and southern edges of the old town as well as flour and animal feed mills towering over historic quays by the waterside. At the same time the Wash port still functioned as a market town and shopping centre for an extensive rural hinterland. An influx of farmers and other country people swelled its population every Tuesday and Saturday as it had for centuries. One bustling traditional community co-existed alongside Lynn's new docks and factories (though its harbour or fleet was lost in the construction of the former): the fisherfolk of the North End. Here at least 85 fishing smacks were based in 1901 when 208 men under 60 identified themselves as fishermen. The town was therefore a fascinating blend of ancient and modern but the election of Frederick Savage as Mayor in 1889 had symbolised a turning point in local history. After 700 years an industrialist rather than a merchant was now chief citizen!

Nearby Gaywood became a town suburb rather than a Norfolk village in 1935 but Lynn's population was still only 25,000 in 1950. A second industrial revolution was now planned by local and central governments to boost the growth of the Wash port and market town. It was, moreover, recognised as a treasury of Medieval and Georgian architecture which needed resources for its restoration. An overspill agreement with the Greater London Council in 1962 started the development of suburban industrial and housing estates. Food, refrigeration, clothing, chemicals and light engineering were strongly represented by the 50 companies offering 5000 new jobs in Lynn between 1962 and 1971. Its population climbed from 28,000 to 35,000.

In 1974 Lynn and West Norfolk had united for local government and in 1981 the Borough of King's Lynn and West Norfolk was created with its own Mayor. Lynn is by far the largest population centre in this largely rural district with about 43,000 in the urban area.

The electrification of the railway line between Lynn and London in 1992 helped to ensure a slow but steady expansion of the town. NORA (Nar Ouse Regeneration Area) is the acronym given to an extensive former industrial area in South Lynn which is being regenerated with housing and business facilities and possibly a marina. On the nearby Saddlebow industrial estate the German company Palm Paper Limited has invested £400 million in building a large paper mill on the east bank of the River Great Ouse. It is Europe's biggest such plant and began production in 2009.

Despite the consequences of its industrial expansion and town centre redevelopment post 1962, Lynn can claim to be a historic town of national significance. Parts of Old Lynn were tragically lost through the building of a new shopping centre and carparks but its historic riverside streets and buildings remain. Its link with the Hanseatic League of the Middle Ages was highlighted in 2004 by the visit of the 1380 reconstructed ship the *Kieler Hansekogge;* then in 2005 the Borough of King's Lynn and West Norfolk became England's sole member of the New Hanseatic League.

In the summer of 2009 the Borough Council organised a Festival to celebrate Lynn's past and present association with the Hanse. Its popular programme featured concerts, exhibitions, lectures and a riverside market with the *Lisa von Lübeck,* a ship modelled on the caravels of 15th century northern Europe, voyaging from the Baltic to England for the first time. Civic leaders from Lübeck, Hamburg and Gdansk attended this grand event which helped to strengthen Lynn's connections with today's Hanseatic cities whose ships were frequent visitors to the Wash port in the 14th and 15th centuries.

A CASE STUDY:

THE MERCHANTS OF ELIZABETHAN LYNN 1558-1603

Until the 1840s Lynn was a river town with good water communication with nine English counties, a harbour facing Europe, and well placed to trade up and down the east coast, above all with London and Newcastle. Wool, corn, wine, coal, timber, skins, ale, salt, tar, fish, butter, lead and other commodities were imported and exported. The town might be aptly described as 'The Warehouse on the Wash'. The corn and coal trade between Lynn and Newcastle became of fundamental importance after 1550, the colliers crowding the Ouse, and most of their cargo of 'sea coal' being taken up river. In the year commencing Easter 1586 a record 18,685 tons of coal was landed at Lynn – or only about 5,000 tons less than London from England's 'Black Indies'.

Corn was even more important than coal. Thanks to its extensive hinterland the Wash port had become *'the great corn market of eastern England'* and it was not unusual *'for her to ship more corn in a month than most ports shipped in a year'*, the conclusion of N.J. Williams. He emphasises that Lynn's exports to Europe were *'very considerable'* but that the coastal trade was the main interest of its merchants. The corn was mostly sent to four main markets or destinations, that is to the Tyne, to Yorkshire, to London and to the garrison town of Berwick-on-Tweed. Lynn's greatest trade was with Newcastle through whose harbour the mining and other populations of the North-East were fed.

The withdrawal of the German Hanse from their business headquarters in the town about 1570 confirmed that London was taking international trade from the provincial ports. But the coastal traffic in corn and coal reflects a commercial revival in Lynn during the reign of Elizabeth I after a slump in urban fortunes all over England. During the 1520s at least 14 ships had left Lynn annually for fishing off Iceland; in the 1540s this was down to 2 but, by 1593, no less than 55 Iceland ships are said to have belonged to the town. Another index of its economic recovery was the return of the February Mart in 1559 following the suppression of Lynn's two fairs by Parliament in 1541. The towns of the hinterland had petitioned Parliament against Lynn because of what was claimed to be *'unfair trading'* or using its geographical advantage to monopolise the herring and other trades. The Norfolk borough was, nevertheless, the port for Sturbridge Fair near Cambridge, the biggest in England, and a great boost to river traffic each September.

From the 1560s Lynn's merchants were erecting new houses and warehouses as well as breweries, with brick the main building material. Before 1600, however, most town mansions were probably timber-framed. The Greenland Fishery in Bridge Street is the latest known timber-framed building in Lynn and was constructed in 1605 as a superior dwelling for John Atkin. Parker emphasises that behind *'all the rebuilding programmes'* was the drive *'for greater comfort and greater privacy'*. The provision of several separate rooms with heating in Elizabethan merchant houses was brought about by the installation of the brick chimney stack. The latter allowed the medieval hall or main living room of the past to be floored-in and the roof space ceiled. Parlours, studies, dining rooms and bedrooms were now far more congenial with their fireplaces and glazed windows. It should be emphasised that many medieval houses in Lynn were not demolished and rebuilt but extensively remodelled such as Clifton House in Queen Street. The Corporation rebuilt its warehouses in brick around the Common Staith, or main landing stage for foreign merchants, and a new market house too.

Lynn merchants were often landlords and brewers as well as shipowners and profits were good. Sailors, coopers, weavers, tailors, carpenters, fishermen, shoemakers, publicans, bakers, tilers (thatch was forbidden in 1572), candlemakers and butchers were all numerous but none so as the now anonymous army of labourers who loaded and unloaded Lynn's ships, boats and carts. Many had their origins in rural East Anglia. Migration from the countryside was a steady trickle without which the urban centres of England would never have grown, for annual births rarely outnumbered deaths within towns. Plague was no doubt the principal reason. It struck Lynn in 1556/8, 1584/5 and, between 1596 and 1599, over 800 burials resulted from it. Plague was a regular mass killer of English townspeople between 1348 and 1666.

The merchant families of Lynn did not escape fatalities in plague outbreaks nor did fathers always have the sons to carry on their dynasties. Hence, the town elite had to undergo social renewal from the migration of merchants from other East Anglian ports, or from further afield. It consolidated its power during the economic and political upheavals triggered by Henry VIII. Dissolution of the monasteries and religious guilds in the 1530s and 1540s created the Corporation estate with the two guildhalls, Norfolk farms, friary sites and riverside property, though the town's economy must have been damaged in the short term by the destruction of religious houses and pilgrimage traffic to Walsingham. The King's determination to sweep away the baronial power of the Norwich bishops was also to Lynn's advantage. In 1537 Bishop's Lynn turned King's Lynn as Henry VIII invested the Corporation with full governing power. Lynn merchants now ruled their City State and, in the Mayor elected annually, possessed their own Doge. An oligarchial constitution which had effectively frozen out the unpopular lords of Lynn, the Norwich bishops, had been granted by Henry VIII in 1524. Twelve Aldermen elected the Mayor from amongst themselves, the latter were drawn from the 18 common councillors whenever there was a vacancy, and these 18 men nominated their sons to succeed them.

Enter Thomas Clayborne and Thomas Grave who were probably the most wealthy of Lynn's merchants in the 1560s and 1570s. The coal and corn trades with Newcastle and London were extremely lucrative. Clayborne and Grave between them shipped 36 of the 178 corn shipments – or over 20 percent – from Lynn to London in 1586. In 1578/9 they handled one third of the total cargoes entering the Wash port from abroad and nearly as many of those leaving for foreign harbours. The Claybornes imported Scottish salt, Bordeaux wine, Danzig pitch, Icelandic cod, Newcastle coal and general cargo from the Low Countries. Corn exports paid the bills but Simon Suckerman of Mildenhall in Suffolk thought that Clayborne got *the greatest parte of his wealth by salte'* and this commodity was very valuable. Lynn's hinterland absorbed vast quantities of coal and wine as well as salted fish. A local shipmaster in 1583 claimed that *'the chiefest parte of the merchauntes lyvinges'* of the town consisted of the wine trade. To facilitate coastal and overseas trade, Lynn's merchants appointed factors or agents in London, Bordeaux, Danzig, Amsterdam and other ports. Grave and Clayborne were naturally greatly dependent on the shipmasters entrusted with their vessels and both merchants owned

four ships with 60 tons the average size. Fortunes made in trade were used to fund fresh foreign adventures and building houses, warehouses, maltings and ships. Farmland in Lynn's hinterland was also purchased. Clayborne and Grave were without doubt two of the most dominant merchants in East Anglia when Elizabeth I was on the throne.

For centuries the merchants of Lynn sat in their counting houses or gazed over the great river dreaming of sons to succeed them and for their families to endure. The eldest son was usually named after the father and inherited the great bulk of his commercial empire. But before 1700 few families managed to last two or three generations because sons were either not forthcoming or died young. Battley investigated 67 Mayors who governed Lynn between 1500 and 1603 and discovered that 55 had migrated to Lynn or died without issue. Forty of these Mayors died before their wives (the average age of death was 55). Thomas Grave had arrived in Lynn from Yorkshire. Lynn's elite needed fresh blood to keep it up to strength.

The origin of the Clayborne family is unclear. A Peter Clayborne was a prominent Lynn merchant in the 1530s living near St. Margaret's and may have been the father of Thomas. If so, his borough freedom should have come through patrimony, because of his father, but it came instead through apprenticeship to George Reveley. The latter was Mayor in 1552. Reveley's wealth had evaporated by his death in 1575 when he was dependent on a borough pension to alleviate his poverty. Thomas Clayborne died in 1581. He had been elected an Alderman before being chosen as Mayor in 1573. His son and heir, Thomas II, received his borough freedom in 1579 *'by reason of his patrimony'* and was Mayor in 1592/3, having been *'elected and chosen'* Alderman in 1585. Thomas II was married at Crayford in Kent in 1599 to the widow of a rich merchant. This was clearly linked to his decision to migrate to London and he was discharged from his position at the Town Hall in 1600. His son and heir, Thomas III, claimed his borough freedom at Lynn in 1622 being *'of London'* and his father simply described as *'deceased'*. The brother of Thomas III, William, went to America in 1621 to serve the Virginia Company as surveyor, secretary and treasurer.

It is perhaps unlikely that the mother of Thomas Clayborne II was still alive in 1622 when Thomas III returned to Lynn. She resided in St. Nicholas Street in 1609 when the annual water rent for *'Dorothy Clayborne's'* house in *'Woolmarket'* is mentioned in the Hall Books. But Thomas I and II lived near St. Margaret's in Stonegate ward apparently opposite the Church with the Great Ouse behind. In 1578 Thomas I had a wooden pipe made from the conduit in the Saturday Market Place to his house (this water was known as *'St Margaret's water'*).

The Clayborne houses near St. Margaret's and in St. Nicholas Street must have been full of people. Thomas I and II would have discussed the import and export trades with other merchants in their parlour. Shops were kept on the premises. Apprentices would have been at hand. No less than six of the apprentices of Thomas Clayborne II were honoured with the borough freedom in the 1590s – Martin Male, Thomas Dege, Stephen Sellie, William Smythe, Osmunde Edwards and John Dangell. The Clayborne wives would have had some influence on this stage where domestic and commercial worlds intertwined. Though Lynn's elite could expect limited privacy at home, their lives were comfortable. Feather beds, good linen, fur gowns and fine furniture ensured that town merchants lived on a par with the landed gentry.

The Claybornes owned other houses in the Tuesday Market Place and St. Nicholas Street where their two shops *'for ye marte'* were to be found. A cottage was purchased in Pudding Lane in 1596. They would have walked from their mansion near St. Margaret's Church to St. Nicholas Street through one of England's major seaports. The wealth generated by trade was being invested in houses, warehouses, maltings and wharfs, especially from the 1570s, a period of economic expansion. It seems certain, for example, that the Claybornes built the warehouse on the South Quay which is now known as Marriott's Warehouse, using stone from the demolished friaries in Lynn as well as brick from local kilns. The dendrochronological evidence tells us that the building was erected or enlarged in the 1580s due west of their house facing St. Margaret's. In this spacious warehouse with cellar, the Claybornes would have stored their corn, salt and wine with the coal stock outside in the yard.

The Claybornes were the neighbours of Sir Robert Bell and later Sir John Peyton who lived at Hampton Court in Nelson Street. Neither was actively engaged in trade to any extent and both were recorders at the borough court as well as holding a seat in Parliament for most of the time they resided in Lynn. Other local gentry and professional families lived in the old town about St. Margaret's Church whilst perhaps the more enterprising merchants by 1600 were based to the north of the Purfleet. At the same time the first medieval town between the Purfleet and the Millfleet still retained a number of Lynn's leading traders and, if the Claybornes stand out, so do the Waldens.

Edmund Walden was a Londoner who seems to have played a forward role in the coastal import of iron into Lynn. He owned several properties in the town and was a cousin to George and Lawrence Walden who were also involved in the iron trade here. This could be the George Walden who lived in Queen Street at today's Clifton House and almost certainly built its tower in the 1570s. He was by now a chief Lynn merchant who had shares in at least three ships and known for *'adventures abrode upon the seas'*. George had eight children, each of whom was left £100 at his death. When he died in 1579 his son and heir, John, was only five years of age and the Waldens' commercial empire was managed by his uncle, William Wullman, to whom the young boy was apprenticed. John Walden died aged only 31 in 1605 and Clifton House was soon in the hands of John Spence who had been an apprentice of George Walden.

The Waldens' home was extensively rebuilt about 1700 by the Taylor family whose mansion overlooking Queen Street is an example of classical architecture, if with a baroque and exuberant porch, but much of the Tudor house remains. During the reign of Henry VIII, the owner of Clifton House had remodelled the medieval property whose southern range or hall was replaced by a new hall and kitchen with a great chamber and bedchamber above. The vast stack and flues of the 16th century kitchen survives. The north and east ranges with their new chimney stacks appear to have been mostly rebuilt in brick too. Probably by the 1520s the medieval house had therefore largely become a Tudor one but building work continued. Blocked windows in the north and west facing rooms of the early Tudor house prove that the double range of two storey warehouses stretching down King's Staithe Lane to the Ouse were constructed later. Of brick, but using stone no doubt from the closed friary sites, these warehouses formed one side of a courtyard whose other buildings have disappeared. All these warehouses were granaries with cellars for wine. At the south-west corner of this commercial complex George Walden later erected his brick tower which was one of several in Lynn in the 16th and 17th centuries. It is of five storeys with mullioned pedimented windows telling of the influence of classical architecture. The stair has a single central newel post and the rooms have fireplaces and wall decoration which was arguably completed during the residence of Thomas Snelling who died in 1623. Though it is clear that the tower was a high status building, it was not directly connected to the polite rooms of Clifton House and its ground floor entrance gave onto the courtyard and quay. In the tower George Walden entertained his business partners and clinched commercial deals whilst it is possible the top room was a lodging, perhaps for merchants from the Low Countries or Baltic.

What is significant about Clifton House is the tower together with its complete historic ensemble of mainly 16th century domestic and commercial buildings, making it unique in England.

Newland, or the second medieval town of Lynn between the Purfleet and Fisher Fleet, was the more dynamic half of the City State, the main landing stage being at Common Staith, to the west of the Tuesday Market Place. King Street was the thoroughfare where most of the wealthiest Tudor merchants bought houses. By 1557 Robert Gervis owned a property on the corner of King Street and Purfleet Quay including a tower. Alexander Musgrave inhabited a house on the site of 5 King Street. He captained the *Mayflower* of 150 tons when it sailed from Lynn to fight the Armada in May 1588. Thomas Clayborne II had lent £20 to the town to help *'the said shippe of warre'* to be equipped and *'sent forth'*. John Dynnesdale lived in today's 27 King Street about 1560 where a tower was built by 1589; John Wallis may have moved into the property later, a Cambridge merchant who shot to prominence in Jacobean Lynn and married the daughter or widow of John Nelson, the ancestor of the great admiral. Next door the Revetts owned a house; they had another mansion in the Tuesday Market Place. Here they held the Corporation accounts for millstones and coal as well as delving into legal business but kept the wheels of their own commercial empire turning. The Revetts take us beyond 1603 into the world of Jacobean Lynn whose merchants have been ably chronicled elsewhere.

Other merchants like John Grebby and William Killingtree had new houses built in King Street and the Tuesday Market Place in the 1570s but did not include shops on the premises. Their breweries and households were supplied with water from the conduit, or wooden pipe, which ran from the Gaywood River into the town. The wealthy

Thomas Sandell lived in St. Nicholas Street where he entertained Sir Walter Raleigh in 1589 and took John Smith as an apprentice in 1595. The latter was to become Captain John Smith in English expeditions to Virginia. Richard Clarke (1535-1601) was Searcher for the Port in the service of Queen Elizabeth as was his son, Matthew (1564-1623). They occupied the property of which today's Tudor Rose is a part and Matthew's daughter, Margaret, married Thomas Snelling of the London Skinners Company who lived at Clifton House. These families have impressive memorials in St. Nicholas Chapel. In 1602 God visited the infection or sickness called the plague on people in one of the tenements of Matthew Clarke in a lane by the beautiful Chapel. Nobody was to approach the house. The common people and their merchant rulers lived close to each other and were frequently threatened by outbreaks of the plague, often with fatal consequences – it did not respect social class.

Hopefully, this essay has shown that Lynn's Elizabethan merchants deserve as much attention as their medieval and Georgian counterparts, being at the forefront of English overseas and coastal commerce. Wealth generated by trade allowed them to invest in houses and commercial properties largely built or rebuilt in brick throughout the reign of Elizabeth I. Though local redevelopment in the subsequent centuries has destroyed much of the Tudor town, the visitor to the Wash port will discover that parts of its urban fabric belong to the 16th century, with Clifton House in Queen Street outstanding. Lynn's Elizabethan rulers were the first generation of town merchants to follow the upheaval of the Reformation of the 1530s and 1540s when Henry VIII dissolved friaries and other religious houses across the nation. The impact on English townscapes was severe and Lynn was no exception as already noted. As if to signal or mark this transition from the medieval to the modern world in the Norfolk borough, the same monarch ensured that even the name of the town itself changed – in 1537 Bishop's Lynn became King's Lynn.

Bibliography

Castleton, F., *Fisher's End* (King's Lynn 1988)

Clarke, H. & Carter, A., *Excavations in King's Lynn 1963–1970* (London 1977)

Gifford, A., *Captain George Vancouver of Lynn* (King's Lynn 2007)

Friedland, K., & Richards, P., eds, *Essays in Hanseatic History* (Dereham 2005)

Metters, A., ed., *The King's Lynn Port Books 1610–1614* (Norfolk Record Society 2009)

Lloyd, T. H., *England and the German Hanse 1157–1611* (Cambridge 1991)

McNeill, J. ed., *King's Lynn and the Fens* (Leeds 2008)

Parker, V., *The Making of King's Lynn* (Chichester 1971)

Pevsner, N. & Wilson, B., *The Buildings of England – Norfolk 2: North-West and South* (London 1999)

Richards, P., *King's Lynn* (Chichester 1990)

Wren, W.J., *Ports of the Eastern Counties* (Lavenham 1976)

Williams, N. J., *The Maritime Trade of the East Anglian Ports 1550–1590* (Oxford 1988)

This title is one in a new series by **Cottage Publications**.
For more information and to see our other titles, please visit our website
www.cottage-publications.com
or alternatively you can contact us as follows:–

Telephone: +44 (0)28 9188 8033
Fax: +44 (0)28 9188 8063

Cottage Publications
is an imprint of
Laurel Cottage Ltd.,
15 Ballyhay Road,
Donaghadee, Co. Down,
N. Ireland, BT21 0NG